IF YOU WANT TO WIN *a raise, a promotion, a big order, a new account, or the best deal in buying or selling everything from a product to a franchise, you need one essential skill to come out #1—and one essential guide to gain it—*

NEGOTIATE YOUR WAY TO SUCCESS

"There is absolutely no doubt that negotiating skills can be taught. We know because we have done it. In the years that we have been teaching business executives and others to negotiate effectively, we have evolved the simple, easy-to-follow techniques you are going to read about in the following pages."

—The authors

ABOUT THE AUTHORS:

DAVID D. SELTZ is President of Seltz Franchising Developments, praised by business columnist Sylvia Porter as the foremost organization in the franchising field. He is also the author of 16 books and nearly 2000 magazine articles on business and marketing.

ALFRED J. MODICA has developed and conducted management and marketing programs for many of the nation's leading corporations, and has served as a corporate officer or director for a number of prominent publicly and privately owned firms. Currently, Professor Modica is Director of Management of the Business and Economics Department at Mercy College and is a director of the Mid-Hudson Institute.

MENTOR Titles of Interest

NEGOTIATE YOUR WAY TO SUCCESS

by David D. Seltz and
Alfred J. Modica

A MENTOR BOOK
NEW AMERICAN LIBRARY
TIMES MIRROR
New York and Scarborough, Ontario

© 1980, David D. Seltz and Alfred J. Modica

Library of Congress Catalog Card Number: 81-81593

This is an authorized reprint of a hardcover edition published
by Farnsworth Publishing Company, Inc.

SIGNET, SIGNET CLASSICS, MENTOR, PLUME, MERIDIAN AND NAL
BOOKS are published *in the United States* by
The New American Library, Inc.,
1633 Broadway, New York, New York 10019,
in Canada by The New American Library of Canada Limited,
81 Mack Avenue, Scarborough, Ontario M1L 1M8.

First Mentor Printing, November, 1981

1 2 3 4 5 6 7 8 9

PRINTED IN THE UNITED STATES OF AMERICA

A Note About Language

Throughout this book we are going to be using the term *adversary* to mean "the person with whom you are negotiating."

We have chosen to do this simply for the advantage of having a single word that can be used instead of a phrase.

The word "adversary" has a meaning that suggests contention or even belligerence. We are asking you to put this connotation aside for the purposes of the ensuing discussion.

In many cases negotiations can be amicable. Since we know that in a good negotiation both sides win, it is possible to have a negotiating session in which the adversary acts like a friend and not like an "adversary" at all. In other sessions, "adversary" might be much too kind a word for the person you are facing.

The point is that we are not using the term in a negative way *or* in a positive way. We are simply using "adversary" as a synonym for "the person with whom you are negotiating."

v

Another problem of language we encountered in the writing of this book was dealing with the possessive pronoun his, and the masculine pronoun he.

In recognition of the growing numbers of women in the higher levels of the business world, we began our first draft by using *his* or *he* or *she* throughout. It did the trick in proving that we weren't sexist, but it didn't read well. So in our rewrite stage the editors insisted that we do some streamlining and use *his* to mean *his* or *her* and *he* to mean *he* or *she*.

We just wanted to take this time to let our women readers know that this is what happened and that although the book reads one way, we both know what we really mean.

Who Can Benefit From Reading This Book

Everybody has to negotiate at some time in his or her life. However, this is *not* a book for everybody.

While some of the principles can be applied to personal situations, this is primarily a book that will teach you how to advance your business or professional career through successful negotiations.

You might be an ambitious corporate employee who has made the decision to "play the game" and rise as high as possible within your company. If so, you will be called on to negotiate your away in and out of many intricate situations as you maneuver your way up the corporate ladder. The information in this book will not only present you with negotiating techniques that you can use to your advantage, but there will be detailed discussion on corporate positioning, a unique concept that will teach you to make sure that you are in the right place at the right time!

On the other hand, you might be an individual who is presently working in a corporate environment, but who feels under-utilized and stifled by the lack of advancement opportunities. If this is the case you are at a crossroads in your life—a crossroads where it is particularly important that you know how to negotiate successfully. Your job now is not only to exit the corporate world gracefully, but to use your skills to get into your own business.

If you are an attorney, accountant, independent insurance agent, architect, banker, real estate broker, doctor or contractor you are in a profession that requires negotiating skill. While negotiating techniques will vary according to profession, the basic skills remain constant and no matter what your profession, you will gain valuable insight by reading about the negotiating techniques of other professions —perhaps of the very professionals that you will have dealings with.

Consultants Negotiating Needs Years ago, the consultant's was an exotic profession. Not so today; as business becomes more complex and as it becomes more and more expensive for companies to hire full-time, specialized employees, the day of the consultant has truly arrived. But this new category of business brings with it new kinds of negotiations. From the initial sale of the consulting specialty to the negotiating of the consultant's fee, the private consultant is almost continuously negotiating with his clients. Since the essence of the consultant's livelihood is long-term relationships with his clients, he must learn to negotiate with an eye on the future—a very special skill that will be discussed in detail.

The main goal of this book is to teach you how to negotiate for the advancement of your own career.

While we will touch on the topic of labor-management and governmental negotiations, this will not be our prime concern here. We will discuss the techniques and applications of top labor and government negotiators, but we will apply them to our primary goal of career advancement.

Finally, we would like to remind you that our knowledge and expertise in this field is continually growing. The material on which this book is based is the result of many hours of field and seminar work —including feedback from our readers and seminar participants.

We appreciate your interest and sincerely hope that you can use the principles discussed in this book to advance your career, increase your knowledge and to enrich your life.

Table of Contents

NEGOTIATE YOUR WAY TO SUCCESS

1.
Introduction to Negotiations

Objectives:

- To teach business and professional people to negotiate for themselves for the furtherance of their careers

- To analyze the true nature of negotiations

- To understand the cooperative nature of good negotiations

This book is going to teach you to negotiate successfully. Primarily, it is about negotiating in the business world. But once you learn the techniques of successful negotiations, you will be pleasantly surprised to learn that these same techniques will help you to negotiate in your personal life as well.

There is an ancient proverb that goes something like this: "Give me a fish and I will eat for today; but *teach* me to fish and I will eat for the rest of my life." This is our aim here. We want to teach you the skills of the successful negotiator, skills that will prove invaluable to you in your career and in your private life.

WHY IS NEGOTIATING IMPORTANT?

If you follow the career of any successful business person, professional, political or academic leader, you will inevitably find a person who is a polished and effective negotiator. With small exception, negotiating skill is essential to success. The reason is simple. No matter what business or field of endeavor you choose, you will be dealing with people. Unless you can get people to see your position and understand your needs, you will not prosper.

It is interesting and ironic that, despite its obvious importance, there has been very little formal training in the negotiator's art. Only recently have the more enlightened colleges begun to develop courses to teach their students how to negotiate for themselves.

Yet there is absolutely no doubt that negotiating skills can be taught. We know because we have done it. In the years that we have been teaching business executives and others to negotiate more effectively, we have evolved the simple, easy-to-follow techniques that you are going to read about in the following pages.

Once you read the book and begin to use negotiating techniques you will be astonished at the resources you never recognized before.

THE KEY TO NEGOTIATING SUCCESS—YOU!

At this point some of you may be skeptical. Is this another one of those books that is going to teach you to win by intimidating your opponent? The answer is an emphatic *no*. But the point is worth considering because many people have the mistaken idea that intimidation, brow-beating or other show of force is the true nature of success at negotiating. If this were true, then heavyweight boxers, middle linebackers and underworld enforcers would be representing us at the United Nations and in corporate boardrooms all over the country. In fact, many of our best negotiators are well under 200 pounds and are physically unexceptional. They get results, yes, but by skill, not intimidation.

Set your mind at ease. You will not have to change your personality to become a good negotiator. In fact, the key to your success is your own personality. Instead of trying to psych yourself up to being someone that you are not, our methods will teach you to understand yourself, evaluate yourself and to use your intrinsic strengths—and weaknesses—to negotiate effectively. We call this method of increasing results "leveraging," and we will talk about it in more detail in later chapters.

Negotiating is a skill but it is also an art. Like all arts, there is a good deal of variation in the methods and practices that can work for individual practitioners. No two negotiators will perform exactly alike for the simple reason that no two negotiators have identical personalities. Since our system is one that depends on the strengths and characteristics of the individual, you will probably not be comfortable with some of the techniques discussed.

As you read through the book, you will find yourself integrating some of the methods and rejecting others. This is fine. Each method is a tool for a negotiator to use or to set aside as he sees fit. You know yourself best and, therefore, you should know better than anyone if you could be comfortable with a particular method. However, a word of caution is in order. Study all of the methods, whether you intend to use them or not. Remember that even though a method might not work for you, it might well work for your opponent and therefore it is to your advantage to know as much as you can about all the negotiating methods discussed.

THE ESSENCE OF NEGOTIATIONS

Like most things in our overcomplicated, computerized society, the true nature of negotiations is misunderstood by most people, and for good reason. Newspapers, radio and television report on the progress of negotiations between unions and management, presidents and foreign ministers or between skyjackers and police authorities. Inevitably, the reporting of these events is colored by the emotion-charged words that the media used to describe them. One side is said to be ready to "cave in;" management seems determined to "smash the union." The skyjackers seem bent on "forcing the hand" of the authorities. Of course, the media have their reasons for reporting in this manner. Their job is to make the news more important and more interesting to attract and keep their audience. Their job is not to educate people on the true nature of the negotiations that they are reporting. As a student of negotiating, you should understand that the true negotiations taking place beyond the range of the microphones or reporters' pads have very little to do with the fireworks that are being reported in the news.

The police officer negotiating for the life of a

hostage knows something very essential about the person with whom he is negotiating. He knows that whatever else, his opponent is a human being and that there is a very human reason why he has arrived at this untenable position. The police officer hears the wild threats and knows that there is a chance that negotiations might fail and the situation end in tragedy. But all this is not the true essence of the negotiations. If we analyze what is happening, we have two people who each want something. The police officer's negotiating position must be based on his communicating to his opponent that he understands the forces that have converged to create the situation. The police officer extends the person in trouble his friendship and a helping hand in return for the safety of the hostage.

ACRIMONY OFTEN PREVAILS

Most newsworthy negotiations between large unions and management are characterized by extreme acrimony and wild charges on the part of the union and management leaders. But, once again, the charges and countercharges do not have much to do with the negotiating process. For example, it sometimes happens that the principals in negotiations really do understand and sympathize with each other and sincerely believe that a compromise position is the only viable solution. Nevertheless, how does a union leader explain to his rank and file without having them think that he has sold them out? Hence, the fireworks. In this case, too, the true essence of negotiation is taking place away from the interesting media coverage. We know this is true because threatened strikes and eleventh-hour settlements are the order of the day and recur with the regularity of the tides. This tells us that the wild threats and forecasts of doom and destruction must be taken with a grain of salt. Each side must flex its muscles and put on a good show, but in the end this has very little to do with settling the issues.

For example, a major city has learned to expect fireworks whenever its uniformed services, particularly its police department, have a labor contract to negotiate. Inevitably there are wild threats of a city riddled by crime, of widows and orphans being abused by vicious criminals, with the implication that it is all the fault of the city fathers who are too hard-hearted to give the police what they want. The countercharges are also stiff with the city threatening to invoke its no-strike laws and implying mass firings and martial law if the police hold to their threats.

Rarely do these pyrotechnics advance beyond the talking stage. After the shouting, the negotiators both know that life must go on and that the doom and gloom will not benefit either side. Each side will go in with its demands up front and the bottom line in its back pocket. Inevitably they will find a common ground somewhere between the two bottom lines and there will be a settlement. Then both sides will shake hands, prepare reconciliation statements and heave a sigh of relief that they won't see each other again for another three years.

THE HEART OF THE MATTER

If negotiations are not settled by wild threats and shows of force, why are they settled? The answer to this question is disarmingly simple but contains the very heart and soul of every situation that requires negotiating. The reason settlements are negotiated is because *the settlement of the negotiations is beneficial to both sides.* That's the story in a nutshell. Somewhere in the middle of all the bad feelings, bruised emotions and wild charges and counter-charges is a solution that will help both negotiators. Skillful negotiators never lose sight of this certainty as they face their opponents and look for solutions.

Looking for a solution that is beneficial to both parties is the key to success in any negotiations that you will enter. Don't look upon negotiation as a confrontation where you will either force your will upon someone or vice versa. This kind of negative perception is not conducive to successful negotiations. Instead of preparing for a negotiating session the way a fighter prepares for a main event, evaluate the situation and proceed as a skilled negotiator. Analyze the facts, analyze the needs and desires of both sides and then go after the solution that will benefit, not only you, but your adversary as well!

Does this point of view make you scratch your head in bewilderment? It shouldn't. While it is true that people and organizations are basically motivated by self-interest, this doesn't mean that people and organizations can live in a vacuum without dealing with the self-interest of others. It is probably true that *if* a large corporation could get away with cutting all employee salaries 50% and not lose any productivity, it would do it. The fact is that it can't be done. Top management knows that it has to treat employees fairly to get them to produce.

More and more today, large corporations are realizing that money alone is not enough to keep an employee happy and productive. There are some very innovative experiments that are attempting to find ways to make a worker's time on the job more interesting and satisfying. These companies are not expending the time and money on these programs because they are "nice guys" with nothing better to do with their resources. They are doing it because they know that it is to *their* advantage to have workers who are happy.

Any business relationship or any relationship that involves negotiations is (at least) a two-way street. Failure to recognize this basic fact is often fatal to the would-be negotiator.

Take the case of our friend Bob. Bob had a position in a company which is generally described by the terms "middle management." To Bob, this meant that he was doing $25,000 a year worth of work, but was earning a salary of only $18,000. Bob was an exceedingly conscientious worker, he was never late and he never passed on his work to anyone else. He was at his desk promptly each morning, took precisely thirty minutes for lunch and often stayed beyond quitting time to clean up any unfinished work. In other words, Bob was a "model" employee. But it wasn't working for him.

Bob noticed that other workers with far less experience were moving up the ladder much faster than he was. The more he noticed this, the more he brooded, and the harder he worked at his job. He took work home, re-organized his files, and turned all of his energies into excelling at his job. But it made no difference. He stayed exactly where he was and worst of all, he was not making himself happy. Finally, he couldn't stand it any longer.

He studied his own work in comparison to others in his department. He was absolutely sure that he was the best and most valuable worker in his group.

The longer he considered the situation, the more certain he grew.

He made an appointment to speak to his boss. He was determined to demand the greater salary and responsibilities that were consistent with his work record. By this time, Bob had convinced himself that he was indispensable to his company and that it had better yield to his demands—or else.

He went to see his boss, but the meeting was not a success. Bob was shocked to learn that his boss had no idea that he wasn't happy on his job. After all, Bob had never voiced any grievances before. In the midst of his negotiations, Bob found himself carried along by his own emotional state. Once he started, he was like a geyser shooting off grievance after grievance. His boss was shocked or embarrassed into silence. So when Bob finally ended his catharsis by saying: "Either things change around here, or you have my two weeks notice," his boss gladly took the second option. Within two weeks, Bob was out of work—a victim of his own inability to negotiate.

Now consider the same situation with another fellow. Let's call him Ted. The difference was that Ted came to us first and asked our advice about how to move ahead in a job that he liked, but where he wasn't adequately compensated or appreciated. We sat down and talked to Ted, noted the essential facts and advised him how to proceed. We explained our philosophy of negotiating to him and arrived at the best way for Ted to "leverage" his way into a position that would make him happy.

This is what we came up with. Like Bob, Ted was a conscientious worker. But like many such people, he was neglecting a very important aspect of his job. He wasn't letting the right people know how valuable he was. Good old reliable Ted was taken for granted, like the office furniture or the typewriter.

Like Bob, Ted too felt that he was indispensable at his job and that his company really couldn't afford to lose him. Unlike Bob, though, Ted realized that nobody is really indispensable and that it was very unlikely that his superiors would advance him on these grounds.

We asked Ted if he felt confident enough in his skills to seek a job elsewhere if he were unable to negotiate what he wanted. He said that he would prefer to stay with his current employers, but was willing to leave if that was what it took to advance his career. Now we had something that Ted could use to "leverage" and we went to work.

First, Ted went to see his immediate supervisor and told him that he was basically happy with his job. However, since his personal obligations were increasing (he had two children ready to enter college), he asked his superior whether he felt that he had reached a dead end, or whether, in *his* opinion, there was a course of action that Ted could take to gain greater responsibilities for himself.

By putting the ball in his boss's court, Ted accomplished two things. He let his boss know that "Old Reliable Ted" had needs to be met. By asking honestly if he felt this was as far as he could go, he actually enlisted his boss as a colleague rather than singling him out as an adversary, as Bob did. After their talk, Ted's superior took greater notice of Ted's work and decided that he was indeed being under-utilized at his present job. At his supervisor's request, a regional meeting was called and a new position in the department was created for Ted.

ENCOURAGE "EASY" DECISIONS

Let's analyze what actually happened in the light of our theory that the ultimate object of negotiations must be a solution beneficial to *both* parties. First, there was Bob's boss being lambasted by a seemingly crazed employee who not only complained long and bitterly but who offered no solution except getting his own way. Clearly (although Bob was a good worker) it would not be to his boss's advantage to have such an individual around. In Ted's case, on the other hand, his superior learned in a straightforward and unemotional way that Ted was a good worker but that he probably would not stay unless he was given more responsibility and a higher salary. When Ted's boss saw things in this way he realized that it would be to *his* advantage to keep Ted; he then created the new position for Ted. By so doing he had a happier employee and a more efficient department.

If negotiations are successful, it is literally true that both sides win! Ted's superior could have acted disinterested and told Ted that it was out of his hands and that he did not have the authority to help him. But then he ran the risk of having to hire and train a new person to replace Ted, who was already a "proven product." Ted's leaving would not only demand extra time and effort on his superior's part but it would have made his department inefficient during the transition period. So while Ted did get an increase in salary, his efficiency and his department's effectiveness increased and as a result *both* sides were better off than before.

Of course, while the results were positive for Ted

and his company, the negotiations did not come about because Ted's employers were "nice guys" who really wanted to see Ted get ahead. This is not the way things happen. Even though Ted's approach was friendly and low-keyed (to match his personality) he made no bones of the fact that he was perfectly willing to leave if it were determined that he had gone as far as he could go. This willingness to give up his job was a very important bargaining point. Had Ted confessed to his boss that he was $5,000 in debt and couldn't survive five days without a paycheck it is very likely that his boss's interest in doing something for Ted wouldn't have been as keen.

To an outsider watching Ted's progress it might seem that all his good fortune came about as a result of a fifteen minute heart-to-heart session with his boss. It wasn't that simple. The actual meeting, which was calm, professional and amicable, didn't take long but Ted had to prepare long and hard for that meeting. He had to prepare his position; he had to decide if he were willing to gamble, and, in fact, if the gamble were worth taking. Then he had to sit down and analyze his strengths and his weaknesses and those of his supervisor. He consulted with us and with his wife. He also talked with friends in the industry to determine if his demands were reasonable and could be met elsewhere if things didn't work out with his present employer.

In short, Ted worked at being a better negotiator. By using some simple rules and applying them diligently, he was able to negotiate a better position for himself.

Now you are going to learn how to do the same for yourself.

Summary:

- This book is designed to teach you to negotiate for yourself in your business or professional career.

- The first step is to understand what negotiations are and what they are not. Negotiations are *not* confrontations in which the stronger side always wins.

- The true nature of negotiations is a seasoned co-operation between two sides both of which have something to gain by coming to terms.

- You need not be brutal or a "tough guy" to be a successful negotiator.

2.
Preparing for Negotiations

Objectives:

- To understand the critical importance of preparing to negotiate

- To stress the importance of understanding that negotiating is a skill that can be learned and practiced

- To instill the importance of research and fact-finding

- To specify the separate steps needed to prepare for negotiations—namely research, self-evaluation and strategy planning

Preparation is probably the single most important part of successful negotiations.

Any good trial lawyer will tell you that a well-prepared case literally "presents itself." It is the same with a successful negotiating session. If the preparation is thorough and well done, the negotiations will proceed smoothly.

Yet despite the obvious importance of preparations, an astonishing number of business people enter into their negotiations fully prepared to "wing it"—that is, to ask for what they want without anticipating that the other person will say anything but *yes*! This practice is not only bad for present negotiations but it is also terrible for future negotiations. In many cases the result of these free-wheeling, shoot-from-the-hip sessions is a complete stalemate; most of the time this means either a job termination or the permanent discontinuance of a business deal or even a business relationship.

The shame of it is that many times, the thoughtless and ill-prepared nature of the preparations actually kill the deal—not the intentions of the negotiators!

Here is an excellent example of the way poor preparation—or no preparation at all—can end a business relationship that was actually beneficial to both parties. Recently it came time for a small publisher that we know to renegotiate his printing contract for the coming year. His printer, rather small as industry standards go, had been with him for three years and had provided satisfactory service. Recently, the small business magazine had been getting more publicity than usual, and as a result the publisher had received several unsolicited bids from competing printers. While the actual cost of printing that was offered to him was basically the same as he was presently paying his old printer, the extra services, preparation, mailing and so forth were significantly lower at the larger printers. The publisher decided to use this as a way to get a better deal for himself with his present printer. There was one charge that particularly stuck in his craw. His present printer was charging him $14/thousand for a mailing process in which a machine placed computer labels on the magazines. The publisher produced three competing bids with mailing charges ranging from $8/ to $9/thousand. "That's almost 40% difference," screamed the publisher. "You're really giving it to me! If you are overcharging me here, who knows how many other hidden charges are in your bill!"

The printer tried to explain that the bigger printers had the mailing facility in-plant but that he had to use a local supplier. The publisher didn't care to listen. "Baloney," he said. "You mean to tell me these guys are in business to lose money? If you can't meet their price, I'm pulling the job." And he did.

In the end this was not a very happy story for our friend, the publisher. He gave his printing contract to one of the large printers who had solicited him. And he did take advantage of the slightly lower costs. But then a peculiar thing happened. He stopped getting the kind of first-class service that he had grown accustomed to with his first printer. The reason was obvious if he had taken the time to think about it. To the small printer, his work was a big deal so he was treated like a big deal. To the large printer, the work was just another job and was treated that way. If a larger, more lucrative contract needed emergency time on the press, it would get it. And if our friend had to wait, that was the way it was.

The publisher complained bitterly to the charming salesperson who had promised him the world to get the account, but was told that it was out of his hands. The salesperson commiserated with the publisher and even showed him nasty letters that *he* had written to the plant manager. Our friend rushed to his old printer ready to eat all the crow in the world if he could simply be reinstated as a customer. But it was too late. The printer had taken on a new magazine and was now running at full capacity. So now our friend has a case of perpetual heartburn and has to make do with uninspired service. And it all happened because he was too "busy" to prepare for his very routine negotiations.

Had he taken the time to research what the first printer's invoice really meant, he would have seen that the printer was indeed telling the truth. He had to charge more because he was small and didn't have a mailing facility in his plant. The point is that had he spoken to other publishers and otherwise done his homework, he could have negotiated a contract that would be to the advantage of both himself and his printer.

KNOW YOURSELF

Knowledge of the field in which you are negotiating is essential, but it is just one of the areas that a good negotiator will research. Just as important as the adversary's field of endeavor is the adversary himself. What kind of person is he? Just as important as that is the question: What kind of person are you? Unlike other areas that you may have studied, there is nothing theoretical about the techniques of negotiating. Either they will work for you or they will not. If they don't, you will have to put them aside and find some that do. This means that your first prerequisite as a good negotiator is to be brutally honest with yourself. Evaluate yourself honestly because in the final analysis you are all that you

17

have! Unless you can do it with the personality that you really have, you can't do it at all.

FORMAL PREPARATIONS FOR NEGOTIATIONS

Let us reiterate at this time that this is a book about negotiating your way to success in your career. Therefore the negotiations in which you find yourself will, in all probability, be less formal than those involving Henry Kissinger, Theodore Kheel or Leonard Woodcock. Your negotiations will occur when you need something to help your career or your business and you must speak to someone who can help you.

In some cases, your negotiations will be formal or semi-formal. This means that you will be meeting at a set time and a specific place to discuss the topic at hand. On the other hand, many of your negotiations will be almost impromptu, conducted effectively and professionally as part of your everyday business life. The point being that, once you learn the basics of good negotiating, you will indeed be able to integrate the techniques into your everyday business life. Of course, you won't be able to prepare your case for an impromptu negotiation, but you will be able to draw on the self-confidence and professionalism that you showed when you did prepare.

What is being stressed here is the idea that negotiations are worthy of separate study and contemplation. They are not something that you can master "like a duck to water." Time and effort are involved, and most of all a belief that the negotiator's skill is valuable to you. Only if you sincerely believe this will you be able to put forth the effort to negotiate effectively.

Let's begin now, formally, to outline the steps needed to prepare for negotiations:

- *Research*—amass as much factual information as you can to back up the case you want to make.

- *Psychological Detective Work*—spend some time thinking about your adversary. What kind of person is he? What are his likes and dislikes? Is he flexible or narrow-minded? Who are the people you know who have been able to deal with him most effectively?

- *Self-Evaluation—Be Honest!*—what are your strengths and weaknesses? What approach in facing the negotiating table will you find most comfortable?

- *Plan Your Strategy*—ask yourself this question: What will happen around me if I get what I want? Will it be positive, negative or impossible? Give attention to the details of the actual negotiation, when, where and how will it be scheduled. What approach should you take? Alternatives? Reevaluation of the goal of your negotiations.

- *Practice*—actually rehearse the negotiations in advance, using another person as devil's advocate. If you make your mistakes in rehearsal, chances are that you will *not* repeat them during the actual negotiations.

Does all this seem like a lot of work to you? Well you're right! You have to begin with the premise that if something is worth negotiating for, it is worth preparing for. Like anything else, if you expect to reap the rewards you must be prepared to invest your time and effort in the preparation.

Later on we will discuss more specific methods of preparation as they relate to success in either the corporate hierarchy or individual business. Now let's talk generally about how you can maximize your results and make the most efficient use of your preparation time.

It is always best to begin, as the wise man said, at the beginning. Take out a clean white sheet of paper and place it on the table in front of you. Now take pen in hand and write down what you would like to negotiate for. Don't hedge. If you are looking for a promotion write down *exactly* what that promotion would be, including salary increases, benefits, responsibility and so forth. If you want to be in your own business, write down (as far as possible) what kind of business. If you're not sure begin to describe the business that you would like to have in general terms at first, but finally in terms that are more specific. If you are a salesman and are negotiating an important deal, write down specifically what you want from the transaction, including lucrative commission, good will for the future or more promising contacts. The point is to be specific. Many people hedge on what it is they actually want; this is a self-defeating and frivolous thing to do. If you have something that you want you will be unhappy until you get it. But if you can't write down what you want, you will *never* get it because you yourself are unsure of your goals.

If it takes you two weeks to complete this first step, don't worry about it. You have to know what you want before you can negotiate to get it!

After writing down your negotiating goal the next

step is to go back to our list of steps and deal with them one by one.

RESEARCH

There is no more helpless feeling than being in a library full of books with no clear idea of how to find what you need to know. Once again, success depends on being honest with yourself and keeping a clear head. Once again, the way to start is at the beginning. Assume that you have decided that you want to be in your own business. Perhaps you think that since you are a very good cook and enjoy cooking, a restaurant might be the business for you. You probably have visions of yourself dressed in your finest clothes greeting distinguished guests at your thriving establishment.

The first thing that you might want to do is to decide if you would enjoy running a restaurant from a business point of view. The quickest way to find out is to go to your nearest business library and ask the librarian for trade publications published for restaurant owners. Trade magazines are probably the best way for outsiders to get their teeth into a new field of business interest. No matter what field you are currently working in or what field you would like to work in, they all have publications which are edited to suit the particular needs of a business person in the field.

The most difficult part of beginning any research into an unknown area is taking the "first bite." By asking the business librarian a pointed question you will get a quick and courteous response. A good business librarian is worth her weight in gold to anyone who has any kind of research to do in any area

of business. Don't abuse that resource by being
vague or lazy. Most business librarians really enjoy
helping you, provided that you meet them halfway.
Ask them questions, but make sure that the questions are based on some forethought.

Once you go through a few business magazines
you will begin to get an idea of what your new field
of interest is really like. Pay attention to all aspects
of the trade magazines—especially the advertising.
Many times the kinds of ads in a magazine can tell
you much more about the nature of the business
than the editorial features. You know that someone
paid to place an ad where it could be seen by a
special group of people.

Another thing that you can do to prepare to enter
a new field is to hire a business consultant. Consultants' fees are generally high, but they are nominal
compared to the money and the time that you can
lose by choosing the wrong direction for yourself by
trial and error.

Make sure that the consultant you choose has experience in your field of interest and comes highly
recommended. Otherwise try an alternative method.
Choose a going business in another area that you
would like to emulate. Call the proprietor and explain your situation. Then offer to hire him as your
consultant. You can learn more talking to a person
who has been through the ropes than you can by
reading a hundred books on the subject. If there are
no conflicts with his business, he will probably be
happy to share his experience.

If your interest is rising higher in your company
and you want to expand your scope in your current
field, the business library is still the place to begin.
Whether your field is marketing, sales, promotion,

management or technical, the resources are there to help you amass factual information that will support you as you negotiate your way ahead.

Once again, do not go in cold. Determine what kind of information you want. Then proceed to either a co-operative librarian or the card catalogue or Reader's Guide. In addition to trade journals, there are many trade organizations which offer newsletters and other forms of communication. Many times your job can be as simple as finding a good book in the field which is authoritative and offers a bibliography for further reading.

Remember that you are living in an age when there is more useful information available than ever before in the history of mankind. The problem is keeping track of what is available and using it to your benefit. It's hard work in the beginning but it's worth it. Whatever your future holds for you, research skills will be valuable to have. You will begin to feel more secure in your ability to dig out facts, and the self-confidence will come to the surface when you begin to negotiate for yourself.

PSYCHOLOGICAL DETECTIVE WORK AND SELF-EVALUATION

Doing psychological detective work requires a slightly less intense frame of mind than researching for facts. In this case there are no real "right" or "wrong" answers but only your perceptions of yourself and your adversary.

The key to success in this part of your preparation is to be as honest with yourself as you can. If you are basically an easygoing person who is easily influenced you are better off admitting it—at least to

NEGOTIATE YOUR WAY TO SUCCESS

yourself. You will be able to use this self evaluation to your own benefit by planning your strategy to take advantage of the fact that you are not an overtly aggressive person. Likewise you must be honest in evaluating your adversary. If you are actually afraid of the person with whom you are going to negotiate, admit it! Only then will you be able to deal effectively. During the actual negotiations you may well have to use tactics that are clearly theatrical in order to achieve certain goals. However, never indulge in the theatrical when you are planning your strategy. At this stage of the game it is most important to acknowledge the truth.

Since negotiating skills are learned, you can begin to practice your approach by thinking back to similar negotiations that you have experienced in the past. Think about them carefully and try to determine what went right and what went wrong. If the negotiations were with the same adversary, try especially hard to determine how this person got the better of you and why.

Try to recall negotiations that your adversary had with other people. Were these persons any more successful than you were? If so, try to determine why. If not, ascertain what behavior pattern was common to both of you.

Think about your adversary from every possible angle. Is he different with family or close friends than with co-workers or employees? If so, try to find a reason. Is your adversary subject to moods; if so, this is a good hint that you should be extra careful to hold your negotiating sessions when he is in an *up* mood. Is there something that makes your adversary happy or angry? Does he react to the time of day, the weather, the performance of an athletic team?

Sometimes you hear people say, "He's a hard one to figure out" or "If I live to be a hundred I'll never understand her." But it isn't true. Any human being can be understood given enough time and effort. Many people don't like to admit that human behavior is so predictable but most of the time it is. Watch for swings in mood in your adversary and try to figure out what triggered the reaction. Is it true that the really great negotiators are great poker players and they make a conscious effort to keep up their cool demeanor? Nobody can play twenty-four hours a day. Sooner or later your adversary will show some kind of human weakness. When it happens make a mental note and write it down. You will find use for it later on.

PLAN YOUR STRATEGY

Once you are comfortable with your evaluation of yourself and your adversary you are ready to enter the "fun" part of preparations—planning your strategy.

Detailed discussions on various strategies will be discussed in later chapters. At this point we are just going to suggest certain avenues of approach that you might use to negotiate more effectively.

For example, let's assume that you have observed your immediate supervisor and you have noted that (a) he is at his best in the late morning, and (b) he is a free-wheeling shirt-sleeve type who gets anxious when he has to leave the work area and wait to see anyone for a formal appointment. You are trying to add a complex new product to your line, but because of the technical complexities, top management has decided that only senior sales personnel with technical backgrounds were going to be permitted to sell this product. You have done some research and determined in your own mind that even though the new machine is complicated, the potential market for it is actually larger than it is for the standard model that you are presently selling. You want to have a crack at selling the new machine and you know that the only possible way is for your immediate supervisor to write a memo for you to top management.

From your observations you anticipate that a formal meeting with your supervisor would make him nervous and edgy. So you decide to conduct an impromptu negotiation by getting your supervisor's attention at the late morning hour and directing it to a piece of technical literature on the new machine. The supervisor's look tells you that he is confused about your interest in a product that you are not handling. You tell him that you are very interested in a special marketing plan inherent in one of the unique capabilities of this machine. You tell him that you have read quite a bit in the trade journals about the competing products and you feel that many sales could be made around this one point alone. The supervisor is impressed by your interest and knowledge. Your request is put logically and is presented as a proposal that is to the benefit of the company. Since you have put some special effort into the capabilities of this piece of equipment, you are the logical choice to put the plan into action. You ask the supervisor to write your memo and, being in a generally good mood and interested and impressed with your point, he agrees.

This is a simple example but it shows how important it is to choose the correct strategy to implement your negotiations. Had the exact same argument been made at a less opportune time of day and during a pre-arranged session, the supervisor might not have gone along with it because he was a man who did not like to call attention to himself and didn't like to go out on a limb for anybody.

PRESENT YOUR POINTS

I think by this time that a very important lesson about the game of negotiations is dawning on you: *the way a point is presented* is more important (in many cases) than the merits of the point!

This fact of life seems to be hard to accept for many people. It probably originates from the American educational system with its fanatic emphasis on the factual as opposed to the communicative aspects of education. There seems to be an inborn belief that if you do your homework the rewards will come to you. Actually, doing your homework is only the first step. You need to know the facts but implementing those facts requires other skills and another point of view as well. Somewhere along the line our system of education has forgotten that behind every fact is a person and to get what we want in life we must learn to deal with people first and foremost.

Strategy planning directly concerns the personality of both your adversary and yourself. It requires brainwork to plan an excellent strategy but it requires intuition as well. If you are dealing with a man who has a reputation as a hard bargainer and you know that you are much more easy going, you have to allow for both characteristics in your strategy. A friend of ours had this experience when he wanted to rent a small store on a busy thoroughfare. The landlord was a man who had a twenty-year reputation for throwing around his pennies as if they were manhole covers. Our friend, on the other hand, was an artist who was renting the store to start a picture-framing business. He did some preliminary research before he sat down with the landlord and learned that the landlord took pride in the toughness with which he drove a bargain. The landlord delighted in beating his adversary and it seemed that he was more interested in the combat than in the final results. Our friend learned that the landlord, nevertheless, rented many properties at low rents to people who he felt were "poor souls" lost in the real world of business.

FEIGNED NAIVETE

Our friend sized up the situation and formulated a strategy. Since there was no way that he could compete with this crafty landlord, he wouldn't try. Our friend decided to "play dumb" in the negotiations. He presented himself as a naive artist who was lost in the world of business and threw himself at the mercy of his adversary—but not before he made it perfectly clear that he could afford $500 a month rent and no more. He didn't want to hear about escalator clauses or options to renew or anything else that was "beyond him." He politely explained that he was an artist, he liked simple things and if he could rent the store for $500 a month on a five-year lease with no fancy clauses or contingencies he would sign. Otherwise he wouldn't because he couldn't afford any more.

The landlord, realizing that he was not going to get a chance to play give-and-take, lost interest in the game. He knew that he could realize a bit more in rent but he told himself that this artist was naive and honest and people like that always pay their rent. So he agreed to our friend's terms and the lease was signed.

Once again the approach was more important than the facts of the transaction. Had a wise guy offered the same rent and indicated by his demeanor that he was forcing a deal, in all probability the landlord would have held firm and demanded more rent. Thus our friend, the artist, didn't win any battle of the egos, but he did get his lease at a price that he thought reasonable.

PRACTICE: REHEARSAL STRATEGY

This final aspect of preparations for negotiations is one of the most important but least practiced steps in the pre-negotiation stages.

Simply, this is the dry-run or rehearsal for the actual negotiations. After you have worked through the previous steps and done all your digging for facts, self-evaluation, evaluation of your adversary, planning your strategies and so forth, the final step is to rehearse the negotiations and try to practice not only the words that you will use, but the facial expressions, the demeanor and the general tenor of the conversation.

The difficulty with practice is that you must have someone to practice with. This person must act the role of your adversary. You have to have a good friend or family member who is willing to put forth some effort to help you in this part of your preparations.

Of course, you will know much more about the

scenario than your helper and so you will have to coach him on the kind of person that your adversary is and the ways that the adversary would probably react to your points. If you can find a helper who is naturally argumentative it will be to your advantage because then you will get valuable practice thinking on your feet to points that you didn't know were coming. In any case, practice is very important *even if the negotiations that you practice are perfectly predictable*. The reason is elementary, yet it is amazing that so few people actually practice before they enter into an important negotiation. There is no such thing as a "born negotiator" any more than there is a born basketball player, actor or anything else. People are born with talent to do any number of things but nobody can be very good at anything without practice. The more practice the better you will become.

If you have any doubt about the need to practice, try this simple test. Get hold of a small tape recorder and record your first simulated negotiation with your helper. Then play back the tape and ask yourself if you can find room for improvement.

If you are like 95% of the people, you will be appalled at what you hear. Yet what you are hearing on tape is exactly what your adversary would have heard if you didn't practice!

Once again, the problem is what we as American citizens have been taught to think of as important and useful. Think how many medical doctors, one of the highest-trained professions in the world, cannot utter a single elegant sentence. Think how many politicians—people who gain their power from talking to masses of people—cannot get in front of a crowd without a speech written by a professional speechwriter. And yet this ability to communicate and to get your point across in an effective and disarming way is within your grasp. All that you have to do is admit to yourself that it is important. Then practice.

Summary:

It is not possible to be a successful negotiator without preparation. Preparation is not easy. It involves a lot of hard work from the initial research to the self-evaluation—psychological detective work and practice.

There is a natural assumption that experience in the field or a natural glibness can take the place of preparations. This is not true. The best negotiators are the ones who prepare best. Only by admitting the importance of preparations and working hard at it can success in negotiations be achieved.

3.
Positioning

Objectives:

- To define "positioning" and explain its role in the negotiating process

- To stress that positioning fills a current need and provides a style of business awareness

- To learn how to position yourself in your own business or career—most advantageously

- To understand why varied job duties are the key to corporate positioning

- To learn the fine art of "gap detection"

Did you ever wonder how some people have a knack for seeing an opportunity and others, with the same advantages, move straight ahead without seeing what was obvious to the opportunist?

In a part of the city where we have our offices there is a corner on which two of the giant hamburger franchises have set up camp. Needless to say, the traffic is heavy on this corner and business is good for both of them. Directly between the two hamburger restaurants was a large store that was recently a variety store. The former proprietors sold everything from tuna fish by the case, to plastic salad bowls to fishing poles . . . everything that they could get in job lots and sell cheaply. Either their product mix didn't suit the neighborhood or the proprietors didn't pay their taxes, but for whatever the reason, this store went out of business and the large store between the two hamburger giants was empty.

Less imaginative and more traditional thinkers would say that the last kind of store to take this space would be another hamburger restaurant. But in fact that is exactly who did take it and at last glance is doing every bit as well as the other two.

This is the kind of phenomenon that causes many people to scratch their heads in bewilderment. After all, the logic of the situation says: "How many hamburgers can you sell on one block in one city?"

But there is another logic at work. The logic of positioning. Instead of taking the prosaic point of view and seeking a corner with no hamburger competition, the entrepreneurs who put up the new restaurant obviously think like this: "There are already two successful franchises on this single block. Both of these companies are well known for their skill in making profitable site selections. This tells me that there are a lot of people in this area who like to eat hamburgers. I think that I will get my share of the hamburger business because unlike the other two restaurants, I use strictly fresh, unfrozen meat which means that my hamburgers are fresher and tastier and that will set me apart from my competition."

Well, that's what the new restaurateur probably thought and that, in fact, is what came to pass. To establish a successful location for his restaurant, the entrepreneur made use of the method that supplied these "positioning" benefits:

1. Provide a hamburger that the other two did not: one that is "fresh and juicy" instead of pre-frozen.

2. Use the competition's advertising and location as an asset to attract prospects to his place.

DEFINITION OF POSITIONING

Positioning is a business technique whereby the business person makes use of strategic timing to fill a "gap" either in the marketplace or the corporate structure. In either case, positioning is essential to success and also to both business and professional growth.

Think about the companies that you know that have "come out of nowhere" to become successful in a very short time. Whether we are talking about *Rolling Stone* magazine, Fotomat Film Processing Service or any one of hundreds of American success stories, there will always be the same common denominator—the successful entrepreneur realized his success by positioning his product uniquely in the marketplace. The wise entrepreneur will position his product by first ascertaining that the market for his product is out there, and then by careful analysis he will discover why the current products are not quite filling the gap in the marketplace.

Cynics will say that good luck or family money or a fat line of credit are the real keys to success in any new business, but history does not bear this out. While it certainly doesn't hurt to have inherited wealth or friends who attended Harvard Law School, having these is no guarantee of success. Ford Motor Company is one of the largest industrial organizations in the world; it has the money and political power to attract any expert in any field of endeavor. Yet it brought out a car called the Edsel, which was so badly positioned in the marketplace that it had to be removed.

Thus, the formula the hamburger entrepreneur used successfully was this: find out where there is a competitive "gap," fill this gap with your product or service and "position" yourself!

Positioning does not simply mean that your timing is right and you are coming to market with a product that isn't presantably available. To be successful at positioning you have to understand the market and understand what will set loose the mechanism to make a consumer take money out of his/her pocket and give it to you. For example, in the early 1960s there was a bowling craze sweeping the nation. Bowling alleys sprang up overnight and the stock of AMF and Brunswick shot into the stratosphere. The American public is exploited in every possible way and bowling was no exception. No fewer than eight magazines about bowling were quickly launched with significant fanfare. Yet strangely enough, none of these projects succeeded. Why? Poor positioning. Yes, the bowling market was hot but a little bit of research would have revealed that bowlers were not readers. Hence, although they loved to bowl, they didn't have the interest to read about their hobby—and they didn't. This is in marked contrast to the current public interest in jogging and running. The market is supporting several running magazines quite successfully, and the difference is the difference between two distinct groups of hobbyists.

The point being made is that positioning is not something that happens automatically. It is a *goal* rather than a method because, clearly, there have been many successful and well-capitalized ventures that have fallen flat on their faces because of a failure to position properly.

FIND CORPORATE "GAPS"

Positioning is also of extreme importance to the individual who wants to move up in the corporate, academic or business world. Just as "gaps" exist in the marketplace, they also exist within organizations. Everybody has heard stories (such as the one of our friend, Ted, from Chapter 1) of a new boy on the block coming into a company and literally zooming past the tired old employees who have been chugging along for years without making any real progress. How does this seemingly "unfair" situation develop? Good positioning. In fact, individual advancement probably makes the best illustration of the successful use of good positioning.

The first bit of muck to clear up on this point concerns the age-old belief, perhaps taught to us in grade school, that advancement reward, in fact all good things, would come to those who turn in the neatest, most accurate test paper. Or put another way, the best workers would get the biggest rewards. Rather than just tell you that this is not true, it will be proved with a simple question. If *you* had an employee who did a perfect job, who worked hard and long and turned out all the work on time—in effect, who made you look good by such productivity—would you (a) advance this person and take the chance of getting a turkey to take his place? or (b) give him a modest raise to show your heart is in the right place but keep him right where he is?

I think that you will agree that very few in this position would give (a) as the answer. The fact that this happens all the time does indeed put a cloud over the textbook formula for getting ahead that you might have retained from school. But does this mean that only the bad workers get advanced and promoted? Clearly this is not the case either, or at least not without some clarification. If a person isn't good at his job and also comes in late, manages to alienate his co-workers and generally creates discomfort wherever he goes, he will not get the promotion ahead of the diligent worker. Our choice here is not between diligence and incompetence. It is a choice between a worker who is single-minded and steadfast and another who is multi-minded and just as steadfast.

Let's assume that we have two men who work in the printing department of a large corporation. One man does the actual printing. He runs the presses, buys composition and film from outside vendors and does all the physical steps to make sure that the printing job comes out well. The other member of the department is a fellow whose job it is to understand the needs of the department, to order the printing. He discusses each job beforehand with the head of each department and he personally arranges for the delivery of each job.

"VISIBILITY" HELPS

Unlike his co-department member, he never has to

stay late to get a job out. All his work is finished during the daylight hours when the other people in the company are at their desks. Now which of these two men would you think would be a better candidate for advancement? Clearly the man who is most visible to the department heads in the company. They might know that there is another fellow actually running the presses but as far as they know, the man they see is "the guy who takes care of the printing." They don't really care who runs the presses—they just want their work when they need it.

You can imagine the resentment of the man who actually runs the presses. In his mind, he is doing all the "real work" yet he is paid exactly the same salary as his co-worker.

It is not that his co-worker is an incompetent employee but that his friend's job is more visible yet *less clearly defined.* In corporate life, the less clearly defined a position, the better the potential for positioning your career.

WHY A TYPIST CAN'T POSITION

A large number of women have grown into corporate executive positions after having served time as secretaries or "administrative assistants," which many people consider a euphemism for secretary. Yet few women (or men) have come up from the typing pool or from positions as a clerk/typist. The reason for this is that the more strictly defined a job is, the less room the worker has to move into a better position. A typist is a position that is very rigidly defined. The employee is expected to sit at a machine and produce typed copy at an acceptable rate. It is very easy to tell if a typist is doing her work well.

The pages of copy are counted, the errors she makes are counted and if the work meets the company's quota she has a job for as long as she cares to do it. In all likelihood she will remain a typist for as long as she is at that company. Even if she is an exceptional typist and can go 150 words a minute with no errors, she will still be a typist. Even if she is paid at a higher rate than a typist who can only manage 75 words a minute she will have to get used to the idea that she has pretty well exhausted her potential at the job.

The secretary, on the other hand, has a much wider range of skills and, therefore, a much wider chance to excel at one or more different areas that can be valuable to her company. True, she will also type, take dictation and do the filing and record keeping for her boss, but inevitably she will be drawn into the actual business of the company. If she is good, she will learn about the business and make decisions on how to make it better. Many corporate secretaries have tremendous power in the corporate structure because the people that they work for have learned firsthand of their skills and loyalty.

Through careful positioning many secretaries have moved rapidly into sales and management positions by employing the skills they learned as a secretary. Of course, the secretaries who were obsessed with their typing and dictation speed rarely moved on to bigger and better things. This brings us to the very heart of the matter as far as positioning goes—it is what we will call "gap detection" or, to use a football metaphor, "running for daylight."

This ability to see the way things work both in society and in a corporate structure is essential to any kind of success. Clearly you must understand what is possible before you can determine if it is possible for you. The secretary who grinds away at her mechanical duties perhaps has some vague idea that doing this will get her some advancement in the company—but she has no *clear idea* of how this is going to happen. The job of being a secretary and the goal of earning say $600 a week are not consistent. This isn't to say that a person who is a secretary can't earn $600 a week within a fairly short time. The smart secretary will look around her, determine who in the company is doing the kind of work she would like to do and earning the kind of money that she would like to earn, and then see how she can position herself to move into that area.

A secretary with this kind of orientation is well on her way to properly positioning herself for a move upward. The first step had to be a clear idea of what she wanted *and* the presence of mind to determine how to use her present position to move her career either at her company or another.

THE SKILL OF POSITIONING

It would be too much to ask that a skill as important as positioning could be yours simply by reading and understanding a chapter in a book. It takes years of practice to position yourself or your company expertly, but you can only develop this expertise by practice and by trying to increase your skills.

The skill of positioning can be broken down into three major steps:

- observation
- timing
- action

All three steps are important both alone and taken together. Patience and timing are very important concepts to understand before you can make a serious effort to become an expert at positioning yourself. If you have a term paper or project to do at school, you can reasonably be expected to do it on time because school is an orderly place and time periods for doing specific tasks are part of that orderliness. This isn't necessarily the case in business. Aside from Murphy's law, which states that anything that can possibly go wrong will go wrong, there are numerous other factors that can result in your being made to wait patiently for your opening. This is very important! You can't force it. Watching a company do business takes the same kind of skill and savvy that the Plains Indians exhibit when they watch a river for fish or watch a forest for game. To the naked eye it might seem that nothing is happening, but the trained eye sees what is occurring beneath the surface. Things move along at their own pace, and it is up to you to detect that pace and to move with it. Many times this will mean waiting patiently for an opportunity, but sometimes it will mean just the opposite. It often happens that things move so quickly that you really have to concentrate to keep focused on what is actually happening. In this case, too, you have to be ready to accept the challenge—even if you would have liked more time to prepare. Timing is important in business, and recognition of the right timing is a valuable skill to have.

THE FIRST STEP IN LEARNING TO POSITION

Positioning is not something that can be learned

immediately. It is more like a way of thinking that must be cultivated as you continue with your career.

However, you will surely not be able to position unless you first have your goals clearly in mind.

Take out a sheet of paper and fold it in half. On one half write down "Immediate Career Goal" as a heading. On the other half write the heading "Gap To Be Filled." Most of you will not be able to fill in the gap immediately. As you go about your business keep thinking of the blank sheet of paper until you can at least put down a starting position.

You can appreciate how important it is to fill in a gap that actually exists. Successful businesses and successful corporate people are those who have been able to detect a need in their immediate business environment and then have rushed in and filled it. Unless a business fills a need it will not succeed. Unless an individual fills a need he will not be successful or happy in his position.

There are many gaps waiting to be filled.

As you are pondering your immediate goals and the ways that you can best achieve them, do not limit yourself to any single chain of thought. Society has many needs and companies can be helped in many different ways. The most obvious way to help your company is by increasing sales or introducing new products or new markets, but oftentimes it is worth more to a company to handle its business more efficiently and, therefore, to make present sales more profitable. In the late 1960s the securities business on Wall Street nearly came to grief not because it lacked business but because it lacked the management expertise and data processing technology to handle a greatly increased volume of business.

There is no doubt that wherever you are now,

whether looking for a business opportunity or working for a company, there are undoubtedly "gaps" that are just waiting to be filled by resourceful people.

Once you have the "gap" within your sights, the next step is to formulate a plan of action—provided of course that the timing for such a plan is right.

EXAMPLE OF POSITIONING IN A LARGE COMPANY

Assume that you are working in the accounting department of a medium-sized corporation. You want to enlarge your scope but you aren't quite sure how to do it. In the course of your work you are continuously annoyed because the same sequences of numbers keep being used for several applications and each time they must be recompiled and presented in only slightly different form. You find this wasteful and time consuming and frustrating and you begin to examine the problem. You learn that not only do *you* feel this way but so do many other people in the department. You do some outside research and learn that there are now small, relatively inexpensive computers available which could make the department run more smoothly by keeping the much used figures in memory and printing them after each different computation was made. In addition you find that this computer system can interface with more sophisticated computers so that the prospect of future growth is allowed. You put together a cost analysis and present this to your supervisor with your recommendation of how this capital expenditure could save the company money in terms of added productivity and the availability of the data in a much handier format. As a result of your "gap" detection you are soon head of your company's new data processing department.

EXAMPLE OF POSITION FOR A NEW BUSINESS

For a long time you have worked as an estimator for a large construction company. You are not unhappy at your job but you feel the need to be independent, to increase your earnings and to do work that is meaningful to you. While visiting the site of a proposed vacation community that your company is building, you are struck by the distance from the community of any substantial population areas. You are also very interested in the proposed size of the undertaking. There will be many houses and many families that need service. You have long considered moving to the country and you discuss your plans with your wife and family. You buy one of the company's homes and arrange with the company to get its cooperation in your setting up in a small contractor and general handyman business. The company likes the idea because you have an inside track knowing the plans and specifications of the homes. And to be sure you will be the only company-sanctioned handyman in the development. Within a year after the opening of the development you have yourself a thriving little business and a lifestyle that makes you satisfied and happy.

THE ROLE OF POSITIONING IN NEGOTIATIONS

For the most part, positioning is generally employed most effectively prior to the actual negotiating session. It is used to secure a stronger bargaining position by enabling you to secure the best position in the marketplace or in your company. The point that we would like to end with is that positioning skill is a goal that you must work at constantly. It will come to you only as a result of hard work and study. You must learn to observe the business climate around you and to investigate the possibilities that are available. Search out "gaps!"

Any business person or professional who has achieved success is a person with a highly trained sense of how to position a career for advancement.

Summary:

- Positioning is the method whereby the individual or employee consciously places himself or his business into position to take advantage of optimum growth.

- Learning to position involves a combination of clear goal perceptions, skillful gap detection and a feeling for business timing.

- Positioning is important in negotiating because a good positioner will find himself a more secure point of negotiating and will therefore be able to negotiate from a stronger position.

4.

Setting the Stage for Negotiations

Objectives:

- To emphasize that even the smallest details of place and time can be important to the success of your negotiations

- To advise or select the place and time and other physical considerations for your negotiating sessions

- To illustrate techniques to avoid distractions

- To learn not to be intimidated by an opponent who sets the stage versus you

In any endeavor of importance it is a good rule not to leave anything to chance. If you study the behavior of successful people you will see that they will automatically pay attention to details that pass the notice of the average person. For example, a skilled salesman trains himself to remember the names of all the people to whom he is introduced. He doesn't do this to show off his memory or because he wants to impress his new acquaintances with his memory. He does it because he knows that if he doesn't pay attention and later on an opportunity develops in the conversation, he will be at a decided disadvantage if he has not remembered the party's name, his position and other important personal details as well.

So in speaking of the importance of negotiations, we can't forget about the details that go into each negotiation. And one of the most basic details is the place and time of the negotiating session.

There are some cases in which the place and time of the negotiations can be the deciding factor. Take the example of the pro golfer who has agreed to donate his time to a tournament which was being played to raise money for the blind. He appeared at the organization's headquarters to work out the details of his benefit match, and he was introduced to his opponent—a blind golfer! The pro golfer was understandably startled. How could he play to win against an opponent who couldn't see? And if he didn't play to win, how could he survive the publicity of losing to a blind opponent?

He decided that all he could do was to offer his opponent a generous handicap. But to his dismay, his opponent rejected this suggestion out of hand. The pro implored his opponent to reconsider. But the blind golfer was steadfast. "It would not be fair," he said. "I want no special arrangements." The pro golfer sighed. He decided that as bad as it would make him look, he would have to go ahead and play the blind man head to head. "But will you at least choose the course that we will play and the time that we tee off?" he asked his opponent. "That is a common courtesy that I would offer any opponent." This time the blind man agreed. He named a local golf course where he was familiar with the terrain. The pro agreed to his choice. "And as for the time" said the blind golfer with a satisfied smile, "we will tee off on the tournament date at twelve midnight!"

Your choice of place and time of your negotiations may not be as critical but it will be important—too important to be left to chance.

CHOOSING THE PLACE TO NEGOTIATE

If possible, it is always preferable to hold negotiations at a neutral location. Full-scale labor negotiations are typically held not in the company's headquarters or union headquarters but in a neutral hotel or meeting hall. The reason is that there is an obvious advantage to the "home team" which can cause resentment to the visitors and which can, therefore, be a detriment to successful negotiations.

Of course, many times it is simply easier to meet on the premises of one of the adversaries. If you are negotiating for position within a large corporation, the meeting will most probably be held in a conveniently located company office or conference room. If you are an independent business person or professional, the negotiations can be held either at your place of business or your adversary's. Of course, there are other considerations. If you are a small independent contractor or consultant working out of your garage or a shared office it clearly would not be to your advantage to show off your lack of opulence to your adversary (in most cases). Therefore, it would probably make more sense to hold talks in their offices or at a neutral location such as a restaurant.

Many times negotiating sessions can be scheduled with the visiting parties calling on their adversary at the adversary's place of business and then proceeding to a location, usually a restaurant, selected by the visitors. If possible find out about the eating habits of your adversary and then select the nearby restaurant with the best cuisine in his favorite area. If you are unfamiliar with your adversary's food preferences, check out your choice first. Don't assume that your adversary likes the same food as you do. Remember that people have different tastes; some observe dietary laws and some might be vegetarians. So if you feel that a restaurant is the right place to meet, tell your adversary in advance that you have made reservations at a specific restaurant and tell him what kind of food they offer. Then ask him if this is satisfactory before confirming your reservations.

Whether you meet in a restaurant or an office or conference room, a few key factors should hold true.

First of all, the meeting should be as free of distractions as possible. If you have your choice of an office with telephone service and a conference room without a phone, choose the conference room. Even though your adversary's secretary has been told to "hold his calls" persistent callers may nevertheless cajole their way through. The only way to be free of this disturbance is to set up in a room where your adversary is out of telephone range.

This is another reason why it is preferable to use a conference room rather than your adversary's office. Generally the office is situated well within the workflow of the company. This means that the day-to-day business of the company will produce many distractions which can interfere with the negotiations.

SEATING ARRANGEMENTS ARE IMPORTANT

Also, if you meet in an adversary's office, you will probably be sitting in a position that suggests subordination. Typically, your adversary will be at a desk and you will be in a side chair, or worse, on an occasional chair that has been pulled in to accommodate you. There is an inherent "one upmanship" here that can be avoided if you adjourn to a conference room where each party is seated around a table, relaxed and ready to concentrate on the subject at hand.

This might seem like an obvious and elementary point but the fact is that getting yourself and your adversary sitting down and ready to talk is *not* a part of negotiations that you can take for granted! If you have reached this far, that is progress and you should perceive it as such.

You will probably remember that when the Paris Peace Talks were being conducted to end the Vietnam War, there was a seemingly endless stalemate until the *shape of the conference table* could be agreeable to both sides. Each side felt that the table should give specific recognition and advantage to specific parties in the talks and, until this issue was resolved, all other issues had to wait and the war continued.

Like the shape of the table and the convenience of the negotiating room, the actual seating arrangement is another detail of negotiating technique that bears attention. We spoke about the inherent subordinate position of other seats arranged opposite your adversary's desk. Some executives purposely arrange their office so that their adversary's are "put down" simply by the position and level of their seat. An unusually low-slung seat will cause its occupant to stretch up to talk thus causing a discomfort and tension that could work to the advantage of the adversary. In addition, there is the natural advantage of the person "looked up to" by the person who is doing the looking!

EQUALIZING A SEATING ADVANTAGE

A friend of ours has a unique method that he uses whenever someone attempts to use this technique on him. He takes the casual approach and sits directly on his adversary's desk! This outlandish act instantly shifts the balance of power his way because his adversary is now in the position of having to look up at him! Without exception the very next thing that happens is that the man at the desk is forced to get up and suggest that they might be more comfortable in the conference room. A more tactful way of accomplishing the same goal would be to decline your host's invitation to sit down saying that you have some trouble with your back and the low-slung seat being offered to you would do you in.

The important factor in adjusting to the seating in the negotiating arena is to listen closely to your own feelings. If you begin to feel uneasy, intimidated or subordinate to your adversary because of the position you are in, act quickly and courteously to move things back into equilibrium. And don't worry about offending your host's feelings. If he is trying to work a technique on you he knows about it—and he will respect your efforts to turn the tables (or chairs) on him.

CHOOSING THE TIME FOR THE NEGOTIATIONS

The time at which the negotiations are held is every bit as crucial as where they are held. Lately there has been a lot of interest and research in the area of biofeedback. Part of this new discipline addresses itself to the times of the day when individuals are at their peak—and their nadir. Of course, there are individual idiosyncrasies but, by and large, the consensus seems to be that most individuals are at peak efficiency at about eleven A.M. in the morning. This is the time when they have digested their breakfast, they are warmed up but not tired and their systems have not yet been dragged down by a heavy two-martini lunch. So if you are like most people, you will be at your peak at this time of the day.

Naturally there are other considerations as well. At the late morning hour your adversary will also be at his peak. This could be to your disadvantage. In some cases, if you were to run on a later timetable, you might be at your peak at about 2:30 in the afternoon. At this point, your adversary might be ready to tire from the efforts of the day. Therefore, if you have discovered this in your research stages, it might be to your advantage to try to schedule your negotiating sessions later in the day. On the other hand, if you know that *you* hit a low point after *you* have lunch and that you will be at the disadvantage, then it is clearly to your advantage not to schedule your talks at this time.

OTHER FACTORS TO CONSIDER IN SETTING THE STAGE

The place of the negotiations and the nature of the business of the negotiators also play a role in determining the best time to hold negotiations. Each business has idiosyncrasies and times of the day in which the work flow increases. If your adversary is in the brokerage business, for example, it will be best to schedule your negotiations either before the market opens or after it has closed. During the peak market hours, customers are calling, activity is going on at the Exchanges and most people in the business are concentrating on that activity. Therefore, unless your meeting is off the premises of the brokerage house and out of reach of any emergency phone calls it would probably be counterproductive to schedule your meeting for this busy time of the day.

AVOIDING DISTRACTIONS

There is nothing that can hurt negotiations as much as disinterest or distractions on the part of one of the negotiators. If you are going to schedule your negotiations for a specific time, you must first ask yourself if there is anything about the time that could cause distractions. Let's assume, for example, that you want to meet with your supervisor to discuss a change in procedure that you would like to see implemented. The most obvious time is after work hours. This is a time when you are both at your place of business and a time when there are no telephones ringing. However, is it really the best time in terms of getting what you want? On examination it turns out that the answer is *no*. What you are proposing is a rather technical point that requires concentration on the part of your supervisor who has been away from the strictly technical end for some years. This means that he would not be able to grasp your point quickly but would have to concentrate. You also know that your supervisor has just moved to a far-off suburb which is serviced by a very unreliable commuter train. You notice that he lives in deadly fear of missing his train home, and you know that if he misses the express, there won't be another one for another two hours. Putting all this data together you determine that it would be counterproductive for you to schedule your meeting for the late afternoon. Your supervisor will be listening to you with only one ear, and you probably will not be able to get your point across. Therefore, you take the initiative and force a meeting earlier in the day. It is true that you have the office distractions to contend with, but at least this way you have an increased chance of getting your point across.

THE NEGOTIATING CALENDAR

Just as the hour of the day is important, so too is the day of the week. Any business person will tell you that it is many times more effective to make calls in the first part of the work week than the last part. After Thursday night, many people just naturally begin thinking about their weekend and oftentimes their work on Friday reflects this loss of interest and concentration. This is less true with people who work for themselves than it is with people who are employed but after a while even self-employed people begin to take on these traits because they have been conditioned to do so by people who work for a salary. If you are an independent manufacturer's rep and you call on ten buyers on Friday and eight of them are busy or out of the office, you soon learn that *your* time, too, can be used more fruitfully on Friday.

Therefore, take the week into account when you plan your negotiating session. Shoot for the beginning of the week and aim for a time that is in the early part of the day. This is general advice. In the end you will be the best judge of the best time for your own negotiations.

Summary:

- A comfortable face-to-face meeting in a congenial setting is not an automatic part of the negotiating process. Rather, every detail of such a meeting must be planned by the skilled negotiator.

- Even seemingly minor points such as seating arrangements, room preferences and telephone access are important and should be considered.

- Special care should be given to removing every possible distraction from the negotiating arena.

5.

The Importance of Commitment

Objectives:

- To understand that negotiations cannot exist without commitment

- To suggest ways to test commitment in your adversary

- To avoid wasting time and effort by cutting short negotiations with uncommitted parties

- To emphasize that there are certain situations that are not negotiable

Before entering into your negotiations it will be a valuable diversion to consider the moral of the story of the chicken and the pig.

The chicken and the pig were friends who decided that they wanted to go into business together. They noticed that fast food was a growth industry and the chicken decided that the best thing for them was to open a bar-b-q rib restaurant.

Initially the two friends were bursting with the enthusiasm of new entrepreneurs; but the day after they decided on their venture the pig came to the chicken and told him of his decision to back out of the deal.

"Why?" asked the chicken. "You were so enthusiastic yesterday."

"Well," said the pig, "I've thought it over and decided to hold off for now. You see, to you this is simply a business investment. But to me it's a total commitment!"

And indeed, it is commitment that is the vital factor for any kind of negotiations. Unless both parties are totally committed to their positions there is no negotiation.

In negotiating for the advancement of your career or business, one of the skills that you will have to learn is how to determine if your adversary is really committed to his position.

Obviously, this is easier said than done.

Unfortunately, there is no quick way to determine commitment on the part of your adversary. This is a skill that you can only learn from experience and even then there will be people who will mislead you about their intentions.

It is unfortunate but there is a sizable army of individuals whose activity in business is totally talk! These are the people who have real estate brokers show them houses even though they don't have the intention or the funds to actually buy anything. Likewise there are people with positions in corporations who enjoy interviewing people even though they don't have the authority to actually make decisions. And most plentiful of all are the individuals in corporations who delight in dispensing advice to outside vendors but who in reality have absolutely no clout to effect anything. Clearly, negotiating with these people is going to be unprofitable because they are committed to nothing except filling the air with meaningless words.

IDENTIFY THE COMMITTED PARTIES

But even people in actual power often are not committed to the issues that you want to talk about. You might have an idea that you are certain will open a whole new market for your company, but you won't be able to negotiate your way into a position to use it because the chief operating officer has a closed mind about your concept. While he has to pay it lip service, he isn't really about to consider it. Many times people with authority are lazy and inconsiderate at once. Instead of simply telling a salesman that they are not interested or that their contracts are already fully committed they will follow the path of lesser resistance and keep accepting free lunches and keep saying they aren't ready to make a decision yet.

Another form of lack of commitment is the notorious "buck passer." It is a fairly natural phenomenon in corporate life for many people to avoid decisions or even avoid deciding who should make a specific decision. Before negotiations can begin it will sometimes be necessary for you to first "flush out" the person who is in the position to sit down with you and negotiate.

If it becomes obvious while talking to someone that he or she is not the right person, or lacks either the interest, the power or the authority to help you, it is best to broaden the discussion to include others. Hopefully the others will include the person with the interest and commitment to talk to you seriously. For example you can proceed this way: "Mr. Jones, I realize that what I am proposing can't be decided by one person and I understand that you will want to advise other of your associates to deal with it. But since it is a rather unusual proposal that I am making I wonder if it could be arranged for me to be there when you bring up this matter for discussion."

The danger, of course, is that the individual you are speaking to does not have enough enthusiasm to pass the word about you. But sometimes he will and sometimes this ploy works.

By and large, however, finding the committed person is a long and hard journey and even a minor victory of sorts.

COMMITMENT AND NEGOTIATIONS ARE NOT INEVITABLE

It has to be said that every situation that you think should be negotiable is not.

Take the case of a young son of one of our close associates. Joey is a junior in high school and he wants to go to college to become a lawyer. To help himself build up a college fund, Joey got a job at a local fast food restaurant. He started with high hopes, but with each day on the job he grew more discouraged and defeated. The manager, a young man not much older than Joey, was very defensive and unsure of himself and took it out on his employees. Hiring was sporadic and often Joey was asked to work long days—during times when the schedule indicated that he would not have to work. And the pay was very low. Even so, Joey persevered and within a short time he was the top employee. He made it his business to know how things worked and he anticipated things that had to be done to make the job easier for his manager. After proving himself, his attempts to negotiate an increase in pay for himself—or even a preference of hours—fell on deaf ears. Even at his tender age it became apparent to Joey that it really didn't matter how good he was. He was to be treated like everyone else. Having come to this decision, Joey quit.

From this point of view there was commitment and purpose to negotiate. But the management's point of view was quite different. In its view, another young man would come along to take Joey's place and that was the end of that.

It has to be said that in the final analysis the experience was very worthwhile because it taught Joey that sometimes the opportunity to negotiate is just not in the cards. Some people much older than he still have this lesson to learn.

Of all the obstacles to business that you will come across, the insincere or uncommitted individual is the most frustrating. He is also the most inevitable. These people are around and they will waste your time and frustrate you to tears—until you learn to recognize them and move on to more productive individuals.

As above, there are no shortcuts to locating these phonies but you can catch hints if you are careful. It is generally true that the hollow can makes the biggest noise. Beware of those people who promise too much or brag too loud or toss around names of famous people. Be watchful of hints like missed appointments, promises to follow up that don't materialize. Most of all, rely on your own inner feelings about those you are doing business with. It isn't much of a program, but it is really all you can do.

Commitment is the key to negotiations as it is the key to success. You can't get anywhere unless you and the person you are negotiating with both have it. So when you are bearing down across the table with someone who wants what you want, don't be frightened.

Summary:

- In large-scale labor negotiations the commitment of both sides is implicit and the motivation to proceed with diligence is built into the situation.

- This is not necessarily true in individual negotiations.

- Since commitment on both sides is an absolute necessity for the very existence of negotiations, care should be taken to continually test the adversary for his commitment.

- Before effort is put into negotiations, it is first necessary for you to ascertain the seriousness of your adversary.

- In many cases there is simply no commitment, and this means that as far as you are concerned there is nothing to be negotiated.

6.
Dressing Up Your Negotiations

Objectives:

- To discuss the use of props and personal attitudes that can be used to dress up your negotiations to build credibility and impact

- To stress the importance of preparedness and documentation in negotiations

Seasoned salespeople often speak of "selling the sizzle, not the steak." The expression refers to the technique of making a sale by emphasizing or "selling" a relatively minor point but one that will be more immediately understood by the client. In like manner, you can put some "sizzle" in your negotiating technique by the skillful use of props.

Make no mistake about it. Most people do indeed judge a book by its cover. This is the reason why so many successful salespeople dress well and drive big luxury-priced automobiles. If you think about it, there is a real validity to this technique.

If you come into a negotiating session dressed in your finest, carrying an expensive leather attache case and perhaps accompanied by a respected attorney or other expert, the effect will definitely not be lost on your adversary. The very fact that you thought enough of the session to prepare so carefully will convince your adversary in no uncertain terms of the seriousness of your intent.

FORMALITY IS A PROP

The props that you use in a negotiating session need not be physical. In a sense, the initial image that you convey is a prop because it may not be the same image that you would use in a more casual meeting. Formality is another excellent prop. Even if you are by nature a friendly and outgoing sort, it will be to your advantage to enter into any negotiating session with an initial air of formality. This formality is important because it gives you room to maneuver that you would give away if you open more casually. For example, if your adversary begins by calling you by your first name and you do likewise, you are shortening the distance between you before you can determine by discussion whether you are really this close! Pace is very important to successful negotiations and the pace of your talks could be severely jarred if you get chummy right off the bat and then have to retreat into aloofness.

There are other props that can be brought into a negotiating session for their dramatic effect. One friend of ours carries a pocket beeper of the type that medical doctors are fond of using. Often he has arranged in advance with his secretary to have him paged at a time when he is involved in an important negotiation. The reason: to stress to his adversary that he is a *very* important person whose time is *very* valuable.

SOME ESPECIALLY IMAGINARY PROPS

Many times the specific props that you will find yourself using will be determined by the specific nature of the negotiations. During the late 1960s the security business was booming. Locks, alarm systems and other security devices were in great demand because of a rising crime rate and the realization of private companies that losses through pilferage and robbery were getting out of hand.

One of the sub-industries that grew rapidly at this time was the training and selling of guard dogs. One of the more successful contractors in this business used a very effective prop whenever he went to a client to negotiate a service contract. Whereas most of the competition would go to the factory or office building clad in cowboy attire and accompanied by their best-trained hound, this fellow, knowing well about the "sizzle not the steak" theory, arrived in a $300 business suit and didn't bring any dogs at all for his demonstration. Instead he hired a few videotape technicians to put together a very effective demonstration tape which explained point by point the program of canine protection that he was selling. He then purchased a portable videotape recorder which he brought on his sales visits—it was an expensive looking piece of equipment that matched his expensive suit.

The effect was magical. The client could now be

sold on the system with his illusions intact. The dogs on the screen didn't smell like dogs and if they lifted their legs at an inopportune moment, it was edited from the videotape.

Another special prop was used by a man who was a very successful salesman of luxury-priced estates. Because he spent much of his time in his car driving clients to see showcase homes, he did most of his business inside the confines of his Cadillac. Consequently, he purchased a mobile phone and used it to call other prospects and homeowners while he was en route. This prop worked in two ways. First it was a very impressive gadget and unusual enough so that most of his clients had never before seen anything like it first-hand. They were impressed at being able to do business with someone who was important enough to have a phone in his car. Secondly, the phone in the car added an immediacy to the prospect of buying a house that wouldn't exist under more leisurely conditions. If things were so active in the real estate market that the salesman had to carry a phone with him then it wouldn't do to hesitate for too long.

Clearly, each specific negotiating session presents the opportunity for specific props to dress up the negotiations. But there is almost always a place for these props in *any* negotiations.

YOUR PROPS PUT THE GAME ON YOUR COURT

In addition to dressing your best and making a good appearance it is a definite advantage to use some sort of prop to help *you* to control the pace of the session. The prop might be nothing more than carefully prepared research notes, or sometimes a blank legal pad and pen. The point is to communicate graphically that you are fully committed to the negotiations at hand. In effect, you are showing your respect to your adversary by the research or preparation that you bring to the session.

As a general rule it is a good idea to hand your adversary something that captures his attention and allows you to lead the conversation. This technique is an excellent ice-breaker in any head-to-head negotiating session as it immediately puts the conversation on common ground—your common ground. You can accomplish this most easily by making a photocopy of your material to hand to your adversaries so that they can follow your presentation. Having something in writing is also important because it tends to save time. In most cases, your adversary will ask you to present your facts in written form. Having them prepared beforehand will serve to pick up the pace of the negotiations.

Visual aids have come to be an accepted way of getting a point across in negotiating and in other sessions that depend upon the interchange of information. Many times a point can be put across with a graph or chart that allows the adversary to *see* as well as to hear the points being stressed. This method is especially effective in showing drastic trends in company earnings, or drastic growth of a particular market or industry. Variations of this prop are standardized loose-leaf binders to be handed out to a group to follow the discussion; stand-up charts large enough to be visible to a group; or statistical information, even computer print-outs, which can communicate by adding the credibility most people have for advanced technology.

If you use this approach you should keep all visual material simple. Use each chart to illustrate only one fact or trend. Also, if you go to the trouble of preparing visual aids make sure that the information upon which they are based cannot be refuted by your adversary. And finally, make sure that the visual aids you use are of high quality and as attractive and perfect as you can make them. Remember that your material is an extension of yourself. If you present dog-eared paper with unprofessional scrawlings you may lose the credibility that you are attempting to achieve.

LOW-COST VISUAL AIDS

You would be surprised at how inexpensively you can add a professional touch to the visual aids that you use. Even if you have only a few sheets of typewritten facts you can make more impact if you place the sheets in clear plastic sleeves for examination by your adversary. This dress-up technique is the usual approach of graphic designers who are paid handsomely for designing corporate logos and other corporate identification pieces. These designers know that they are being paid not for a physical product but for their talent—still, there is the need in most people to "feel" the value of the item they have purchased. While, in fact, the designer may get paid for a few strokes of his pen, he will present his drawings lavishly on expensive construction board often with custom diecuts to window his art work. The art work is exactly the same as if he would have handed the client a sketch on a piece of bond paper but the presentation is different and unique. The buyer feels important because this visual extravaganza is for him alone. Again, it is the sizzle not the steak that has changed hands.

The final prop to be considered is an expert or consultant in your field of endeavor. It is commonplace for a buyer and seller of real estate to be represented by an attorney at a closing, likewise for an experienced accountant to be close at hand when a business or franchise is bought or sold. There are many other instances in which it is acceptable and sensible to have an expert at a negotiating session.

If you are buying real estate it might be very helpful to your case to have a professional engineer accompany you if there is a structural or deterioration problem that could seriously affect the selling price. Union negotiations for better working conditions have been known to produce doctors and other scientists to testify to the effects of certain work environments on the worker. The person who is investing money in a field that is not known to him is indeed foolish if he proceeds without the aid of a consultant who is an expert in the field.

Naturally, bringing someone with you who is not directly involved in the negotiations per se is much different than bringing a chart or loose-leaf binder. While there are times when an experienced negotiator might want to make use of the element of surprise, in most cases it is still best to ask your adversary if an expert can accompany you at the negotiating session.

Finally, remember that you are dressing up your negotiations for a reason. The idea is not to bring physical props to impress your adversary—all that you are attempting is to enhance your credibility and effectiveness through the use of props. Props can help but they are, after all, only props. Don't make the mistake of many conscientious people who lose track of the forest for the trees. Your goal is *not* to develop overwhelming props. Your goal is to become an effective and skillful negotiator. Props can help you but they are only one part of your overall campaign.

Summary:

- You can increase your negotiating effectiveness simply by dressing the part.

- Aids to successful negotiations should be relevant and meaningful. Make use of high-quality, easy-to-understand props.

- It is often valuable to think of formality and self-confidence as a "prop."

7.

The Use of Leverage

Objectives:

- To define comprehensively the negotiating technique called *leverage*

- To suggest ways of using the leverage technique

- To illustrate successful use of leverage by means of case histories

- To stress the importance of prudence in the use of leverage

In business, the term *leverage* means the ability to get multiple benefits from the assets that you actually have. For example, a company with leveraged stock simply means that the shareholders are using borrowed money to increase the fortunes of the company. It is called "leveraged stock" because the debt increases the capitalization of the company but does *not* increase the equity ownership. Therefore, the stock is theoretically more valuable because these same owners now have more money to work with than the dollars they initially invested.

Likewise the term *leverage* is often used to describe the activities of speculators who invest heavily on margin. This hardy crew borrows money to make investments in either the stock or commodity markets. Because they are using borrowed money, they can buy more shares or more contracts and, hence, their prospective gains will be greater than if they purchased only the investment they had the cash to secure. Of course the risks are also greater to the leveraged speculator but that is the reason to play that game to begin with.

The use of borrowed money to escalate financial success is part of every major individual success story from Aristotle Onassis, who used borrowed money to finance his first cargo ship, to William Zeckendorf, the famed New York real estate tycoon, who leveraged his way to billionaire status on a mountain of mortgages. The field of endeavor might vary but the basics of leverage is constant throughout: the speculator secures himself a position in a ship, building or other asset by putting down a small amount of cash and assuming existing liabilities. He then finds someone to refinance the deal taking a profit for himself while maintaining control of the property. He uses the profit to buy one or more new properties and continues the same game.

In each case, the successful user of leverage is getting advantages far in excess of the actual investment that is made.

This same principle can be used in the world of negotiations. If you leverage your strong points skillfully, you can gain benefits that might surprise you.

THE SECRET OF LEVERAGE IN NEGOTIATIONS

The way in which leverage can be used successfully in negotiations is illustrated magnificently by the story of the ugly moneylender and the merchant's daughter. These days personal bankruptcy has become an increasingly popular method for individuals to shed old obligations with a minimum of pain. In fact, new liberalized bankruptcy laws have been revised to make the process even less painful and humiliating than before. But it was not always this way. Debtor's prison was a reality not too long ago, and this is the time in which our story takes place.

It seems that a merchant in merry old England had the bad luck to owe a large sum of money to a moneylender. Business was down and the poor man found it impossible to repay his loan. This would mean not only personal ruin but also a long and lonely stay in the local debtor's prison. However, the moneylender proposed an alternative solution. He suggested that if the merchant would give him the hand of his beautiful young daughter in marriage, he would cancel the debt in return.

The moneylender was old, ugly and of unsavory reputation. Daughter and merchant both were aghast at the suggestion. But the moneylender was clever and suggested that it was only fair to let Fate decide the matter. He put forth the following proposition. Into an empty money bag he would place two pebbles, one white and one black. The daughter would reach in and select one pebble. If she chose the black pebble she would marry him and her father's debt would be forgiven; if she chose the white pebble she would be free to stay with her father *and* his debt would be forgiven. But, if she refused to choose a pebble, the deal was off and her father would go to debtor's prison.

The merchant and his daughter reluctantly agreed. And the merchant bent to pick up the two pebbles to put into the empty money bag. Out of the corner of her eye the daughter saw the crafty old man had selected two black pebbles. It appeared that her fate was sealed.

You will have to agree that she didn't appear to be in a very strong bargaining position. True, the moneylender had acted unethically, but if she exposed him she was back to square one and her father would go to prison. If she didn't expose him and selected a pebble, she had to marry the ugly moneylender.

This was clearly a time for the application of a little leverage.

The girl in our story was beautiful, but she wasn't empty-headed; she knew herself and she knew her adversary. She knew that she was dealing with a crafty man who would stop at nothing to get his way. Also she knew that there was no way to match wits with her adversary face to face. No, the ultimate solution would have to come with her playing the role of the sweet and innocent young girl.

When the moment of truth came the girl reached into the bag and selected a pebble, but before its color could be determined she fumbled the pebble and let it drop onto the roadway where it became instantly indistinguishable from the other pebbles in the path. "Oh my goodness," exclaimed the girl, "how careless of me. But no matter, sir, all we must do is look at the color of the *pebble left in your bag* and this will tell us the color of the pebble I selected!"

Checkmate. By carefully evaluating all the factors involved and determining a strategy, the girl negotiated herself out of a perilous situation and into a position of advantage. Having set this stage for the old man, she knew that he would not be able to go back on his word and admit that he tried to cheat her. So as a result she was able to return home with her debt-free father.

The girl in the story succeeded because she wasn't afraid to change the rules of the game after she determined that the rules as they were written would not be of any use to her. In short, she turned her disadvantage into advantage by looking at the bigger picture.

It goes back to the point we made in the first chapter. The only way to be a successful negotiator is to make full use of your own personality complete with all your own strengths and weaknesses. Truthful self-evaluation is the key to the successful use of leverage. And the key to truthful self-evaluation is a maxim that first became popular among the practical philosophers of the Middle Ages: Paraphrased slightly this maxim states that "to have a good life, it is good to learn to make a virtue of necessity."

All this means is that if you have a certain character, admit it and use it to your own advantage.

A few years ago the financial community was dazzled by the salesmanship of a man named Glenn W. Turner. The flamboyant Mr. Turner built a quick empire with an organization that he called "Dare to Be Great" in which he used the sales skills he had developed to teach others to believe in themselves and be motivated to make huge sums of money. Mr. Turner began his notable career as a door-to-door sewing machine salesman in the nation's Bible Belt. And he started with a serious problem for a door-to-door salesman—he had a very distinct and glaring harelip. He quickly capitalized on this disadvantage by making it part of his sales pitch. "I see that you're looking at my harelip, ma'am" he was known to say to his prospects. "Heck, it's just something I put on this morning so a pretty lady like you would notice me." Mr. Turner was clearly a very successful salesman and though his product line changed, his approach never did. He sold himself along with each product, harelip and all!

Another part of leverage is to maximize your efforts and not to waste them in unproductive gambits with your adversary. Many people who are in the position of negotiating for a job begin their quest with two strikes against them because of a resumé that includes too many points that are not applicable to the position that they are seeking. Don't be afraid to be an editor in your negotiations. Be selective in what you choose to use. The negotiation process is above all a communication process, and it does you no good to heap on irrelevant or misleading factors that only serve to confuse the main issues.

AN EXAMPLE OF RESUMÉ EDITING FOR LEVERAGE

After a career as a schoolteacher, a friend of ours decided that he was ready for a change and determined to make his way in the business world. He was an effective schoolteacher, a mathematician, and a resourceful fellow who could have helped any number of companies in any number of ways. But no one wanted to give him a chance. It didn't take our friend long to see he was doing something wrong. So he changed his approach. It was clear that even though he knew the skills that went into being a good teacher could be applied in a commercial setting, his prospective employers did not. At his last position he was assigned the title of assistant principal. At the small-town high school in which he taught the title was largely ceremonial. He featured the title and although it took only 5% of his time, he devoted 95% of his resumé to talking about the administrative and leadership duties he performed. He went into detail about his dealings with school unions, employees, and suppliers—all true. Then he let the resumé reader draw his own conclusion.

Within a month of using his new approach he had a job. He used what little he had to leverage his way to a position he wanted. Industry had a prejudicial way of looking at teachers. He presented himself in a way that wouldn't arouse that prejudice.

Our friend is now working for a large beverage company and he is doing very well. This is an opportunity that he would never have enjoyed if he had allowed the company to take him at face value.

LEVERAGE AND ANALYSIS

In order to leverage with your strong points, you first have to isolate them and make sure that they are crystal clear to you.

Let's assume that you are negotiating for the sale of a house. You are buying a house that is in less than tiptop condition. The price already reflects this, but you feel that you can make a much better deal. You know that there are others interested in the house but you feel that you are in a unique position.

You are buying the house not as a residence but as an investment—an investment that was strongly recommended to you by your accountant because you need tax deductions badly. While it is perfectly true that a person buying the house to live in is just as interested in the selling price as you are, such a person will be more interested in other considerations—such as the beauty of the floors, walls, paint color and other items.

In addition you know that the house is presently financed with a standing mortgage—an instrument which requires only interest payments plus a small amount of principal each year with the balance paid in a balloon at the maturity of the mortgage. Such a mortgage would not be of much value to most homeowners who would probably choose to secure their own financing. On the other hand, this type of mortgage would be beneficial to you and it would have the added benefit of being transferred to you on the sale, thus speeding up the transaction considerably.

You take these leverage points into your negotiations with you. The owners of the house want to retire and therefore they want to conclude their business as quickly as possible. However, like most homeowners, they are emotionally attached to their property and feel that it is worth more than it is. You enter a bid a few thousand dollars lower than their asking price. You tell them that you would like to meet their price but that you calculated the cost of the cosmetic changes that were necessary to put the house in shape and they brought the price of the house to a few thousand *over* what they are asking. Therefore you are doing the fair thing and splitting the difference with them. You then quickly end the discussion and tell them that of course they will want some time to consider your offer. By planting the idea of renovation costs in the owners' heads you are giving them something to worry about with the buyers that are going to be bidding against you. The owners are now unsteady in their conviction of what their house is really worth. The probable effect of this is that you will get a phone call accepting your offer.

TURNABOUT IS FAIR PLAY

The jujitsu approach is part of the leverage technique of negotiating. It involves using your opponent's strength to your advantage. Simply stated it means that to get the results you want with a strong adversary, don't try to meet him head on. Like a skillful matador, get the bull heading in your direction, but before the moment of impact step deftly out of the way and let your opponent's momentum work for you.

At the simplest level this jujitsu technique can be used effectively if you are entering negotiations with a very loud, abusive, or abrasive adversary. These individuals, for whatever reason, are always spoiling for a fight and their conversation is very aggressive and pushy, as if it will prove something to have them dominate the conversation.

The worst thing that you can do against such an individual is to play his game. All that can come of this approach is bad feelings, raised blood pressure and possibly worse. The best way to deal with this situation is to use your opponent's great strength against him. Don't get baited but instead tell him calmly and firmly:

"Mr. Smith, I can assure you that I came here to

do business and not to fight with you. I think we have some important business to do, and I know from your reputation in this field that you don't like to waste time. Why don't we complete our business first, and we can fight later if you like."

By turning the other cheek you will completely disarm your aggressive or obnoxious opponent and, if there is any commitment on his part, you will be able to get down to business. Always remember, too, that many people believe that the way to win is to come on so strong that their adversary is terrified. In effect the aggressive behavior may only be an act. But in any case, your approach should be to hold your own ground and be yourself. Remember, no business deal is worth losing your dignity.

LEVERAGE CASE HISTORIES

Using Leverage to Get an Account: A young management consultant was hard in pursuit of a major utility company which needed help in compliance with new environmental laws. The young man made a good impression and was clearly on the ball, but he was forever receiving the same objection: "I'm sorry but we only do business with established firms." After a few discouraging sessions the young man came up with a way to leverage away this objection.

"Mr. Smith, I can understand your policy and I am sure that if I were in your shoes I would have a similar policy. But I want to point something out to you. No large consulting firm that you can hire will be able to do as good a job on this project as I can. Here's the reason. It is a brand-new field and my degree is one of only 56 granted throughout the entire country. If you look at the letter that the State Environmental Commissioner wrote concerning my dissertation, you will see that although I'm still young I did indeed write the book in this field."

The consultant knew that rules are made to be broken, and he had enough sense to know how to use his advantage to greatest benefit.

Using Leverage to Overcome Hostility: Salesman Ted Hoffman was making his annual trip to a large pharmaceutical firm to talk about updating the computerized billing system that he had sold them last year. When he walked in he was greeted by an openly hostile department manager. Rather than meet hostility with hostility, Ted let the manager get it out of his system, and he expressed surprise and shock at the treatment that he had received. He opened up his folder and pointed to an official-looking computer sheet.

"Sir, I haven't the record of one single complaint. I don't know what's going on around here but I hope that you will let me get to the bottom of it."

The department manager went on to explain that the new machines should increase their efficiency at billing by over 50%, yet this turned out to be untrue. These expensive new machines were actually less efficient than the old manual way of doing things and the durability of the old machines was better, too, as they didn't require the frequent sales calls. Ted was baffled by the statement and asked the manager if he could have his permission to view the machines being operated.

He didn't have to watch for very long before he detected the problem. The whole purpose of these machines was that customer information would be fed into the machine on a tape and then billing information would be keyed in. The operators were keying in all the information. In effect they were using the computerized devices as a typewriter. The problem came about when the operators who were trained by the company left for higher-paying jobs. The operators who took their places were never properly trained, and the operators that *they* trained were even less so. Ted called his home office, explained the problem and received permission to stay at the site for two days, thoroughly training all the operators at the company.

The results were so dramatic that Ted came back with orders for two additional keyboards and a word-processing system that interfaced with the existing equipment.

Thus by relying on the confidence Ted had in his technical knowledge, he turned around a customer who started out as his enemy.

Using Leverage to Overcome Emotion: Bob Blank recently went through a rather traumatic divorce. He felt bitter and wronged by his wife's actions and was being very unreasonable about the alimony and child support payments that the judge was ordering. The judge, an older man with quite a few years of experience in the situation, asked Bob: "I know how you must feel about your ex-wife. But let me ask you this. Do you have any feelings for the welfare of your children?" Bob said that he surely did. "Well then, do you have any reservations about the ability of your ex-wife to provide a good home and care for the children?" Bob admitted that his wife was a good and competent mother. "Well then," said the judge, "let me show you something." He then took out the classified section of the local news-paper and turned to the section on domestic help. "Let's assume that your wife were not on the scene. You are a working man so you could not take care of three young children. You'd have to hire a babysit-ter, a cook, and a housekeeper. Now suppose you just make a rough estimate of what that would cost you." Bob was stopped dead in his tracks. He had never thought about the situation in this way. "An-other thing. You are in business so you know that just because you pay someone to do a job doesn't mean that it will be done well. With your ex-wife on the job you are relieved of that worry." Bob quickly agreed upon the stipulated payment and walked out of the courtroom feeling not that he had been fleeced but that he had made a shrewd business deal.

In this case, the judge used the leverage of com-mon sense. By appealing to facts and figures, he forced Bob to put aside his emotional view and to see things his way.

Using Leverage to Overcome Reason: Business people often assume that most people are reasonable and, as a rule, most are. However, there is still room in the world for those who are completely beyond reason. In fact there are some people who actually manage to take advantage of their very irrationality.

It became increasingly popular in the 1970s for young, predominantly professional couples to buy large old houses in the inner cities of America. The advantages were the generous living space, the low taxes relative to suburban living and the proximity to the life and resources of the city.

In one so-called "brownstone belt" in New York, many of the new homeowners got involved with restoring their homes to their pristine states. This meant repairing oak doors, mating oak and cherry-wood moldings and doing other feats of carpentry that might be required.

A beneficiary of this trend was a Jamaican cabinet-maker named George. Unlike his American contemporaries, George was trained on hardwood, and he handled it expertly and quickly. As a result he had all the work that he wanted, and he was able to get it at his own unreasonable terms.

George could look at a job and estimate exactly what it would cost including his time and materials. He then insisted that he be paid in advance. Many of the new homeowners were young lawyers whose pride couldn't tolerate a business arrangement such as this. They offered to pay for his materials and wanted to pay the remainder on completion of the job to their satisfaction. This drove George crazy.

"Your satisfaction! What do you know about woodworkin'. My friend, nobody's a harsher judge of work than old George, and that includes you."

George then went on to state in his own direct way that he had literally hundreds of recommendations of satisfied customers. All of them paid him in advance. Therefore if you wanted George to work for you, advanced payment was the condition. Incredibly these wheeler-dealer lawyers would inevitably go along with these very unreasonable demands. George was good and he was reliable. In the end it made more sense to deal with his irrationality than to hire someone else who didn't have his reputation for craftsmanship.

Of course George didn't even know that he was negotiating. In his mind he was just doing what was fair and right. At the start of his career, a customer had refused to pay him and George decided that this would never again happen to him. Because he was possessed with a very special skill at a very special time, he was able to use leverage to overcome rationality.

THE BOTTOM LINE OF LEVERAGING

Leveraging your adversary for an advantage is a powerful negotiating technique. Like any powerful tool it must be used with care. If you do maneuver yourself into an advantageous position, you should never abuse your advantage. Instead you should approach your goal comfortably, again with the attitude that what has transpired will be good for your adversary as well as yourself.

For example, you are bargaining for the sale of a piece of real estate, and you know that the owner must sell because of pressing needs. The recent changes in the tax laws concerning inheritance taxes, for example, has made it necessary for many people to liquidate properties in order to pay their taxes. Whatever the reason, if such an advantage comes your way, take advantage but do not abuse your adversary. No good can ever come of one individual feeling that he or she has been "had" by the other. Even though the deal might be signed and sealed there is always the possibility that your callousness or lack of tact can come back to haunt you. Never run down or humiliate an adversary over whom you have an advantage. Be gracious and respectful, and under no circumstances allow any kind of business transaction to be taken personally by your adversary.

Isn't it better to say, "This is such a fine old house and I really wish I could afford to pay you what it is really worth. But my budget allows this much and no more" than to say, "Let's face it you have a problem with this junkpile. It's about to fall over and it's going to take an army of high-priced mechanics to put it back together. Now you have my offer—take it or leave it!" Of course it is better. And the difference in approach won't cost you a cent. As someone smart once said, "It's nice to be nice."

Then too, there is another caution. While it is true that everything is negotiable, it is *not* true that every negotiation has a final solution. There is such a thing as pressing too hard and you have to be very careful that you don't pass that point.

Even a desperate seller will balk if the offering price is too low or if the demeanor of the buyer is too insulting. Most lawyers are pragmatic people, and if they can solve a problem by negotiating out of court they will usually attempt to do so. However, if the amount of money involved makes it worthwhile to litigate, you can be sure that they'll be there lead into battle by their bluebacked papers and process servers.

A friend of ours is a collection lawyer. His goal is to try to get a creditor to pay back *something*. He knows that collecting money with the help of the courts can be done but it is a slow process and then, too, in certain cases, even after a money judgment is handed down the assets will have to be found and attached. Therefore our friend proceeds at his task with extreme friendliness. He knows that the numbers favor him if he gets all of his accounts to pay something, even if it is a small amount. However, this doesn't mean that he will *not* pursue a creditor who does not co-operate. He knows that after a certain amount of effort, it is pointless to continue being reasonable and negotiations break down to the tune of a summons. Naturally, since even collection lawyers are human, if he feels abused or offended by the attitude of an account he might lower the legal boom that much faster.

Always temper the goals of negotiation with reason. Or put another way, sometimes it is better in the long run if you leave from the dinner table just a little hungry.

Summary:

- Leverage in negotiations is the technique of using a small advantage to obtain great advantage.

- The use of leverage demands that the negotiator have good self-knowledge as well as the facts pertaining to the negotiations at hand.

- Leverage is a powerful negotiating tool and it should not be overused lest the effort be counterproductive.

8.

The Push-Push-Pull Theory

Objectives:

- To define and explain the "push-push-pull" theory of negotiations

- To stress the importance of give-and-take in negotiations

- To present illustrated cases to aid reader comprehension of this technique

THE PUSH-PUSH-PULL THEORY

This negotiating technique falls more into the category of an overall principle than a specific technique.

Just as the skillful fisherman learns that he has to "play" his catch carefully, first setting the hook, then letting the fish run with it before applying a little pressure of his own, so does the new negotiator have to learn that the over-all tempo of good negotiations is always push-pull, never slam-bang.

An overpowering or ramrod approach to negotiations isn't effective because it doesn't recognize the position of the adversary. There are no negotiations in a dictatorship or in a prison camp. In those places there are only raw authority and those who have to succumb to it. In the negotiation arena there are always two sides, both of which have input into the negotiations. This is the reason why the push-push-pull theory is so important. It is the process by which you can get what you want while maintaining a relationship of respect with your opponent.

THE PUSH-PUSH-PULL IN ACTION

The push-push-pull theory also helps build strength into the negotiations by keeping them from appearing to be too one-sided. For every gain that you make, you should give something back to your adversary, even if it is something that is little more than formality. For example, at a recent session that we heard about, two attorneys were squabbling over the terms of a lease for a commercial property. The terms were for a net lease in which the tenant would pay the taxes and the heat but the tenant's lawyer was insisting that the landlord install a new and more efficient boiler and insulate certain key parts of the building to assure that the tenant be able to control his costs.

The tenant's attorney cleverly pointed out that it was a buyer's market and that his client was willing to walk away from this deal if the landlord didn't come to terms on these key points. The landlord's attorney knew that the tenant's attorney was absolutely correct. There was no scarcity of available space, and he advised his client that it would be in his best interest to make the required capital improvements. However, the landlord was a man who had nothing but bad luck with this building which had remained empty for the last twelve months. He was very hesitant to "throw good money after bad" as he said. The two attorneys got together and discussed the situation. The tenant's attorney came back with this proposal: he was still insisting upon the new boiler and insulation, however, he would take it on a month to month basis with his client paying for the improvement initially and taking an amount out of the rent on a month to month basis until it was paid back. This satisfied the landlord and the deal was made.

The reason for the success was a push-pull effect used by the attorney for the tenant. He took a hard line insisting on what he wanted, but then he softened on how this demand was to be delivered. He pushed, and pushed, but before he pushed too hard he softened and pulled the landlord in by making the deal more attractive to him.

Of course the push-push-pull can be delivered as pull-pull-push as well. Sometimes the situation calls for the technique to be used in reverse. A divisional vice president whom we know was recently recruiting a hard-driving sales manager to boost up his division's performance. He spared no expense in flying this talented man all over the country, meetings at expensive resort hotels and the complete V.I.P. treatment. He was pulling pretty hard using all the sugar that he had available to lure his catch. But the vice president didn't get to where he is by being naive. At the precise time when he thought that his target was getting comfortable and confident in his negotiating position, he arranged an interview with another hotshot in the industry for the same position. He made sure that his man knew about the meeting. The employment contract was signed before the pampered fellow could even think about getting too big for his britches.

As with other aspects of successful negotiations, the single most important aspect of the push-push-pull theory is that you have clearly in mind what you want and what you can afford to give up. It is perfectly all right to camouflage what you really want if you think that it will help you realize your goal more quickly.

KNOW YOUR PRIORITIES

Let's assume that you are negotiating with your supervisor to redefine your role in the company. If your supervisor is like most, naturally he will assume that this means that you are after more money. This is possible, but it might be that you are a person who takes the longer view of things and what you really want is to re-align your duties to make them conform with your perception of the future of your field. In your case, let's assume that it means concentrating more on the technical aspect of the machine that you are selling and de-emphasizing your time at prospecting and entertaining new clients. You realize that the short-term results will mean a loss of business. The move is absolutely essential as you feel that a change is going to come over the business which will render much of the current hardware obsolete. You enter negotiations with your real goal the realignment of your priorities, but you also have as a bargaining position the fact that you haven't had a salary review for over a year.

Therefore you decide to push-push on your salary demands first and then back off. When you do back off you substitute your real goal as a substitute for money. If you have properly evaluated the goals of your supervisor as keeping the payroll within 7% of last year, you will probably come away from the session with a complete victory—a modest raise and the time to get more deeply involved in what you consider the more important part of your job.

DOING WHAT COMES NATURALLY

Negotiators must integrate the push-push-pull technique into their very natures. It has to be as much a part of you as your smile or your handshake. It is like a tennis player's forehand—an essential and central part of the game. By practicing the push-push-pull you will eventually be able to feel the rhythm of success which should then begin resounding through all your negotiations. It is a rhythm of give and take which should signal that you are becoming expert at one of the most important games in business.

A refinement of the push-push-pull is to learn to instantly identify the parts of a deal that are unimportant to you and to dress them up and give them to your adversary as if they were gold. A crafty old attorney friend of ours uses this story of how he closed a deal with a gift that he would have had to give away at distressed prices anyway. He was selling his little summer house and could sense from the give and take that he was very close to closing. He was pushing hard for his price and the buyer and his wife kept hemming and finding possible objections. Our friend backed off the negotiations and asked the young man to help him put his canoe into the water and then instructed the man to take his wife for a boat ride to discuss the matter privately. When they returned he didn't wait for them to speak but announced that he was going to give them the canoe as a gift because they looked like they had so enjoyed it.

After all the hard haggling over price the young inexperienced couple fell for the bait hook, line and sinker. It was a handsome canoe and one that would cost them quite a penny if they went out to buy it. Our friend the lawyer knew that the canoe was much more valuable to them than it was to him. First of all the market in used canoes was soft and it would be a nuisance to place ads in the paper and entertain prospective buyers. This was after all a summer house and his primary residence was in the far off city. And of course, there was the more obvious fact that if he didn't give the young couple his canoe with such a grand gesture, he would have ended up leaving it with them anyway.

However, to the couple looking forward to enjoying a house in the country, that canoe represented a large chunk of money that they would not have to spend. So the transaction was made and both sides came away winners—or thought they did!

PUSH-PUSH-PULL TECHNIQUE
USED TO NEGOTIATE AN IMPORTANT SALE

Ed James is a highly motivated salesman of photo-typesetting equipment. He has been his company's leading producer for the past two years, and he shows no signs of easing up. He is high-powered but not pushy. His technique is to talk to his customers most important need: the ability to compete favorably in a highly competitive business. Ed comes equipped with numerous articles, charts, and statistics proving that the quality and reliability of his equipment far surpasses the machinery manufactured by his competitors. In addition he points to the larger share of the market that his company is managing to land each year; this is especially important because the more of his equipment in the field the more trained operators will be available. This is important in a field that depends on skilled help.

Ed is relentless in the way that he piles on the benefits. It almost takes the client's breath away. But this is only the first stage of his sales strategy. The sale is really closed not on the push-push but on the pull. Ed accomplishes this by asking the client what is keeping him from giving him the order. The answer is most always money. The customer explains that to lease this more expensive piece of equipment he would have to increase business. Ed counters that he will be able to increase business more easily because of all the features and conveniences of this new machine. At last he lands the final blow softly and moving away from his push direction.

"These machines are four months back-ordered; unless you order now you will never get delivery for the busiest time of the year. I tell you what I can do. Give me your order now. At least I can then put in the order. If you change your mind I guarantee that I will refund your down payment, even if the machine gets delivered; you can still send it back and it won't cost you a cent. Meanwhile, if you decide that you want it, at least you'll have it when it can do you the most good."

Let's analyze what has happened here. The customer has been pushed hard to consider the benefits of a modernized piece of equipment. In most cases the customer is well aware of the benefits and really doesn't even need to be told. This occurs because phototypesetting is a technologically intense industry where machinery and capacity can be rendered obsolete very quickly. The customer is thinking hard all the time he is being barraged with benefits: "I really would like to have that baby in here, but who can afford it?" So when Ed offers the no-obligation order, it is irresistible to many customers. He knows that it is a rare customer indeed who sends back a piece of machinery once it is delivered. His sales records bear out this perception.

Summary:

- The overall direction of negotiations is never in one direction only. The "push-push-pull" theory is no more than an odd-sounding name for the give and take that *must* be a part of every successful negotiation.

- In negotiations the shortest distance between two positions is never a straight line!

9.

The Money on the Table Technique

Objectives:

- To describe the "money on the table" tactic in negotiations

- To caution the overuse of this technique

- To illustrate by case history the way that this technique works

The "money on the table" concept is a handy method to steer the negotiations into more fruitful directions. It serves to clear the air and to re-establish the fact that you mean business.

In the classical sense the two adversaries are haggling across the negotiating table. The discussion is heated, but it is evident that there are more words in the air than there is intent in the hearts of the participants. Finally, in exasperation, one of the arguers stands up and bellows, "If you really mean what you say, let's see you put your money on the table!" His adversary has no choice but to clearly define and express his position, and the negotiations can move forward.

The "money on the table" concept is a powerful tool for moving negotiations along in the right direction. But it should not be overused. Remember that every negotiation is a human inter-action as well as a business meeting. While this doesn't mean that you should litter your session with small talk, it does mean that you will achieve your goal more quickly if you decrease the intensity of the negotiations by occasionally moving the conversation "off" the money. If you bear down too hard and deal only with the important issues, it might have the effect of hardening the negotiations and giving your adversary the impression that you are unwilling to be reasonable. Perhaps more than anything else, the "money on the table" concept can serve you best as a timesaver. We spoke earlier of how important it was to have a commitment on both sides of the negotiations. But using this method you can find out quickly enough if your opponent is serious or if he is just playing with you.

A small publisher that we know had this unfortunate experience. His small magazine was well positioned in a specialized area of business, but like many smaller publications, he was under capitalized. His magazine was managing to break even each issue but he didn't have the cash to work on his circulation and distribution to make the publication irresistible to advertisers. The problem was money. Printing costs had escalated so dramatically that he just couldn't free any working capital to enable him to improve his position. Enter a salesman from a large printer. He made his pitch for the account and told the small publisher slyly that his boss had a record of financing new magazines, but that, of course, this had to be strictly on the hush hush. The reason he gave made perfect sense.

"We have 100 magazine clients," he said. "If it becomes common knowledge that we invest in magazines we will be swamped with requests from everyone who gets into a cash-flow problem." The salesman proposed a deal in which a value was to be assigned to the common stock of the small magazine. The first six months' print work would then be paid in magazine shares. At the end of the six months the publisher could either buy back his stock at a pre-determined price or he could let the ownership of these shares remain with the printer. The deal sounded fair to the publisher and he had a midnight session with his accountant to get ready for his meeting with the head of the printing company. A deal like this one was just what the doctor ordered because it would remove the month-to-month pressure of the printer's bills and allow the publisher to work on building a firm financial base.

KNOW YOUR FACTS

At the meeting the printer dug into the financial records of the magazine with great interest. He interrupted his meeting to call in the head of his accounting department. They caucused together and finally left the room to talk in private. The printer returned and asked more intimate financial details. At this point the publisher had no choice but to ask his adversary to put his money on the table. "Mr. Jones, I have kept my end of the bargain; I came to you and made full disclosure. Now are you going to accept my payment in stock or aren't you?" The printer seemed to ignore the comment. He took out his pencil and did some hasty figuring. "If you give me $5,000 down and assign your advertising revenue to me, I'll put you on press. Otherwise I can't extend you any credit. Your books show that your business is too shaky." It suddenly became evident to our friend that he had been suckered. The salesman had set him up for a financial fine tooth comb in the guise of making a possible investment. By using the money on the table concept he didn't make any headway in the negotiations but he did learn that there *were no negotiations*. And this was well worth discovering before more time and effort was wasted.

On the positive side, the "money on the table" concept can be used as an aid to closing a deal. This method works when an adversary, sensing success, comes forth with an additional inducement thus sealing the deal instantly. Consider, for example, the case of the two men who were negotiating for the price of a house. They had been going back and forth for about a month. It was one of those situations in which both sides knew that the deal was uniquely for them. The seller knew that his house had rent-controlled tenants—which was definitely a disadvantage in the market because he couldn't legally remove them and they were paying very low rents legally. The buyer was also in a unique position. He was actually representing two buyers who were going to buy the house together. Since a bona fide owner could legally evict a tenant if he were going to use their apartment for his own use, these buyers were in a unique position to get a very good buy on the house. Both sides knew this and they gradually moved closer and closer together. But eventually both sides tired of the game. Negotiations came to an end for almost a complete month. During this time both sides had time to reflect. The seller received no serious interest on his property and the buyers found nothing even close to their price range. Mentally both sides decided on a bottom line. The buyer called and made the offer, prefacing his quote by stating that it was final. The seller on his side said that he too had a final figure in mind. He suggested that it might be simpler if he simply stated the lowest price that he would take. Upon disclosure the buyer sighed and said that they were still $1,000 apart. Without even a moment's hesitation the seller rushed to put his money on the table. "I'll tell you what I'll do. We're $1,000 apart. I'll split the difference with you if we can come to terms *right now!*" The buyer, who was also tired of the long negotiations, agreed, and the deal was made immediately.

ESTABLISH CREDIBILITY

A final point about putting your money on the table. When you say that you are going to do it, make sure that you mean what you say. There is a time for bluffing in negotiations, but it is more important that you build a reputation for being a credible and reliable business person. Success in business means repeat business, and repeat business means that you must have credibility with your associates. If you renege on terms after you have "put your money on the table," your adversary may possibly forgive you, but he or she probably will never forget what you did.

Deceit, and trickery have no place in your negotiating repertoire. Even if you can achieve your goals short term by being less than truthful, you will lose out in the long run, and this is just bad business. Also, by being forthright and ethical you have the right to demand the same from your adversary. In the long run, that is a decided advantage for everyone concerned.

MONEY ON THE TABLE CASE HISTORIES

The money on the table concept is also a very good method for "coming clean" with your adversary. Structured correctly it can communicate to your adversary that the time for playacting has gone and you are offering what is in essence your best deal.

This is shown graphically in the story of two garment district workers. Sammy is a cutter with a reputation as a man who likes a good deal. Bennie is a salesman. His regular line of products is fabric, but he will sell anything that he can. Indeed, it could be argued that it is the selling and not the product or even the money that motivates Benny.

One day Benny came to Sammy with a deal that was too good to pass up. "Sammy, I got a deal for you that you wouldn't believe."

"Oh yeah, what have you got?"

"An elephant. Unbelievable! A pedigreed, African elephant. And for you only $1,000!"

"Sorry, Benny, I have no use for an elephant."

"Sammy, I knew you were going to do this to me. Okay, $750 and that's my final offer."

"Look, Benny, I am a cutter. I work on 21st Street

and I live on 86th Street. What possible use could I have for an elephant?"

"Five hundred dollars and I'm giving it away."

"Benny, I don't want your elephant. Now please, I have work to do."

"Sammy, I'm putting my cards on the table: I'll make it two elephants for $500!"

Benny looked up from his work with a satisfied look on his face. "Two elephants," he cried, "now you're talking!"

The money on the table concept works well in more common situations too. Consider these brief examples:

Example I: A paper salesman is calling on a local printer. He is selling a 13,000-pound odd lot of a very expensive, coated paper. The printer states that he recognizes the value but that he has no need for the paper just now. The salesman puts his "money on the table." "Look, I have to sell that paper in a hurry. If you give me the order I'll only charge you for 12,000 pounds and the other 1,000 pounds will be a bonus to you." The money on the table clinches the sale.

Example II: A young couple has purchased an old barn for conversion into a restaurant. They are negotiating with a painter to complete the interior and exterior decoration of the building. They know that the painter is good because he comes to them highly recommended. However, his estimate is a full $1,000 more than any of the competing bids. The couple decide that reliability is worth the extra money but they want to be sure. They tell the painter that they will agree to his price—but only if he puts a time of essence clause in his contract. This means that he would forfeit a percentage of his price if the work was not completed by a stated date. Not wanting to lose the job, the painter agreed to reschedule some of his other work and came to terms with the young couple.

Example III: A young lawyer just beginning his own practice makes constant use of a local stockbroker for information about the value of securities on the date of death for his clients' estates. In many of the estates, however, the stocks were not kept with this broker, and he got nothing for his services. So when the young attorney made this request again the broker balked and voiced his discontent. The young attorney put his money on the table and in no uncertain terms. "I'm a young fellow, just starting out, and I do all my business through you. Now it might be that it doesn't pay for you now, but you can certainly look to the future, can't you? I understand your point, and I will understand completely if you no longer want to render this service to me. But if you don't help me now when I need the help, I promise that I will take my business to somebody who will. You know that you have a certain investment of time with me already. So it's up to you." Looking upon it in this light the broker decided that the young attorney did indeed give him all his business and that it really wasn't his fault if it wasn't more. He decided that the time it took to help was an investment in the future and was worth making. But it took a sharp negotiating turn to make him realize this.

Summary:

- Putting your "money on the table" indicates a

commitment to a specific negotiating position in no uncertain terms.

- It is a technique which forces the adversary to understand your position clearly and to act on it.

- This is a powerful tactic and a final one as well because if it is used without forethought it might well have the effect of ending the negotiations before they run their course.

10.

Know Your Out!

Objectives:

- To emphasize that a negotiated settlement is not always the best course of action for you

- To teach that in some cases it is possible to "negotiate yourself right out of business."

- To show how half a loaf is sometimes not worth the effort

- To emphasize that integrity in negotiations is far more important than coming to a settlement at any cost

While it is important to be optimistic, the successful negotiator must also learn to be realistic. There is not a successful end to every negotiation—sometimes things just don't work out, and the best way to absorb this setback is to convince yourself that those ventures that didn't work out actually did work out to your advantage.

WIN BY LOSING!

Indeed, it is often true that in negotiations you can win by losing. How many stories have you heard of the go-getter type who upon being denied a modest raise by his boss goes off and starts a successful competitive company? If things had gone smoother they never would receive the push they needed to get started. Also, many business deals never get off the ground because the chemistry is wrong from the beginning. In most cases these stressful deals, like bad marriages, are better off going unmade.

After a while you will begin to feel viscerally when something is not right for you. This is an unscientific approach perhaps but one that will have to do until something more useful comes along. If you get this feeling then don't go on with the negotiations. Simply draw your line and don't step an inch over it. As you will see, often it is better to accept half a loaf—and occasionally no loaf at all—than it is to enter a deal in which you don't feel comfortable.

Take the case of a fellow we heard about who wanted to go into his own business. He found a man who wanted to sell his business and retire. The two arranged to meet to talk about the possibility of sale. The buyer is very affable and friendly; he is experienced in the business and the seller feels very comfortable discussing matters with him. The buyer doesn't flinch at the asking price. In fact he offers no resistance at all. They meet a few times and each time the buyer pays for dinner or lunch. The seller is feeling very good. He knows that the buyer knows this business, and he makes sure to show him how strong his location is and how loyal his clientele. But before they conclude their agreement, the buyer tosses a monkey wrench into the works.

He will agree to the seller's price but he won't agree to *any* cash payment on closing. He will make higher monthly payments in the form of notes, in effect paying the seller with proceeds that he takes out of the business. These terms come as a shock to the seller, but the buyer makes a persuasive argument. This is a service business and experience is important. What good would it do the seller to find a buyer with cash but without the skills to run the business? Then too, if cash were paid up front, this would have to reflect in a lowering of the selling price which would result in unproductive and possibly acrimonious haggling. No, there was no doubt about it. He would take the deal and commit himself fully to his business. But no cash up front!

The seller was deflated. He had expected a quick and easy deal and mentally he was already retired and at leisure on a southern beachfront. For this reason he was disappointed because he knew that he could never live with a no-cash agreement. He called the prospective buyer and told him that he agreed that it would be to his advantage to have a knowledgeable man like himself take over. He stated that even though the buyer was a good man and an honest man, he couldn't live with the idea of selling his business and getting only a legal promise to pay notes on a monthly basis. He implored the man to at least make an effort to pay a token amount of cash, just to show good faith. "I am giving you my business," said the seller. "Can't I expect you to give something to me?" But the buyer wouldn't budge. It was just his way of doing business he said. The seller sighed and hung up the phone. In his heart he knew that he would have to look for another prospect. Later on he found out that he had acted correctly by following his instincts. The buyer had succeeded in buying a similar business for notes and had to turn it back in less than a year.

So while the seller had to get out of his negotiations, he actually accomplished it at great advantage to himself. He stuck to his guns, and after giving the buyer every possible alternative, the man still would not agree to commit himself financially—even to a token amount. By refusing even a token cash payment, the prospective buyer was, in effect, telling the seller that he was unwilling to make him any commitment at all—except his word. This action gave the seller an indication of what that was worth.

DON'T NEGOTIATE YOURSELF OUT OF BUSINESS

The point of this story is that you should not be afraid to either break out of negotiations altogether or be willing to compromise your initial intent. Do not make negotiations into a personal grail that you must carry and win at all costs. If you do, you will wind up with heart trouble, high blood pressure and heartburn. And you will not negotiate as effectively as you would if you were more even-tempered and relaxed.

The fact is that many deals are just not meant to be. In fact *most* deals are not meant to be. This selection process is part of business, and patience is definitely a virtue to be cultivated.

Do not look at failed negotiations as a defeat or a failure. Often you will win by losing, and in any case it won't do you any good to brood about lost chances. Try to learn all you can from each negotiating session but forget about the old do-or-die attitude. It won't do you any good and will probably hurt you.

We ended the last chapter by speaking about the importance of building a reputation for being ethical in all your business dealings. This is a good time to reiterate this point. We have said earlier that there is an element of show business attached to most negotiating sessions. To reach your goal you and your adversary are both expected to do a little bit of "acting," however you must be the one who must know when you are acting and when you don't want to act.

Sometimes you are going to have to take a half a step backwards in negotiations when you would have liked to surge forward. It might be because you don't really have an asset that you wished you did have, or it might be that you are offering something that you can't really deliver. The temptation is always going to be there to exaggerate yourself out onto a limb. Don't do it. The "over extended protagonist," the character who promises too much, misrepresents too much or simply talks too much is probably the favorite stock character of television situation comedy. These shows do make a valid point about misrepresentation: once you step out on one limb it is often necessary to cross over to another limb to further save face. One thing leads to another and before you know it you are yards away from your true objective—separated by barriers that you yourself have constructed. Remember, once you lose credibility, you will find it almost impossible to regain it again.

The central character of J.D. Salinger's novel *Catcher in the Rye* commented on the tremendous influence that the movies have on people's lives—

even without them recognizing it. The same thing is true today, and even though it seems obvious, it is well worth your while to analyze why you feel a certain way—especially when the way you feel flies in the face of logic. All of us have Walter Mitty fantasies from time to time. When we are small we are football players and celebrities; as we get older we tend to fantasize about being like people with other areas of expertise.

If we are drawn to business it is probably inevitable that we fantasize that we are real sharpies who can get our way in any business dealing with only our cool and our sharp wits. It isn't that people like these don't exist—they probably do. Just as the novice writer is advised not to try to emulate Shakespeare, so should the novice negotiator not attempt to emulate the world's great wheeler-dealers—or worse, the image of the wheeler-dealer portrayed on the silver screen. Jean-Paul Belmondo, Paul Newman et al. have highly paid screenwriters standing behind their every word. You will not have this advantage. So don't be reckless. Even if you can make a few points by stretching the truth, practice restraint and let the points go by. You will be stronger and quicker in the next round if you don't have to remember what you *think* you told your adversary in a moment of weakness.

THE HALF A LOAF THEORY

In his recent discussions of the progress of a major New York City newspaper strike, labor mediator Theodore Kheel told an interviewer, "We have solved most of the big issues; the problem is that now the minor issues have become big issues." And this is how it always is. Once you have reached agreement the negotiations can move on to another topic. For this reason it is sometimes smarter in the long run to concede early some particularly sensitive point. In this way you can piggyback your success on this acrimonious point to an overall success in the wider negotiations. Obviously the concession has to be something you can live with but many times you can get more nutrition out of a half a loaf than you can from insisting on the whole thing.

KEEP YOUR PERSPECTIVE

American people have a winning philosophy. Maybe we carry over too much from the sports arena to the business arena, but the fact is that the metaphor of winning is not the best way to enter into a negotiating session. The reason is that for every winner there is a loser, and this distorts the entire purpose of negotiating and negotiations. It is this motivation to win over everything that makes it hard for many negotiators to take their out. However, it is an absolute necessity for success. A smart horseplayer will never bet all nine races. He knows that the factors for success may only exist in two or three races, and that's all he will bet. He knows that if he bet all nine he would probably lose most of them, so he stands pat. In the same way, you have to learn that sometimes winning can be defined as backing off or sitting one out.

Because you are playing the business game for the long run, you should take special pains to recognize your inability to back off. It is a dangerous trait because if unchecked it will inevitably lead to your taking your business relationships too personally.

When this happens you are in a perilous position because you are likely to lose your temper or assume that you are indispensable or attempt to play God. All of the above are danger signals and require that you readjust your thinking to conform with the actual business world. For the plain truth is that *anything* that you do in your business dealings that undercuts your credibility or ethics *will* work against it. The *reason* why you undercut yourself doesn't matter at all. Your business associates won't care that success is very important to you, or that you had an unhappy childhood, or that you have to prove something to your mother, your father or your children. All they will remember is that you went too far, promised what you couldn't deliver and that will be the end of those persons as valuable business contacts.

Therefore we will end this chapter where we began it; by stating once again: Know Your Out! Sometimes you can win by not winning!

EXAMPLES OF INDIVIDUALS WHO DID NOT KNOW THEIR OUT

I. Keith Holiday was a salesman representing a firm that specialized in contracting with businesses for the use of temporary help. He had made a contract with a firm that had a tremendous need for word-processing operators. Keith's firm represented many individuals with typing skills, some of whom were college educated. He knew that they were not really qualified, but the contract was too fat and he couldn't resist stretching the truth. He made a note to have the firm's personnel department see what they could do about training the typists that he was going to send over to operate the client's machines. Keith was counting on good chemistry developing between the workers he placed and the management of the client company. He knew that his people were selected because of their basic skills and their appearance and personality. He was sure that they would be able to master the machinery in good time and he would have an account that would keep his commission check healthy.

But that's not what happened. The client company appreciated the fact that the people they were sent were sincere and good workers, but they greatly resented the misrepresentation. "If we wanted trainees why would we have to come to you?" was the plaintive cry. Keith lost out two-fold. The word-processing people were all let go and the other office people who were legitimately placed by Keith's agency were also replaced. The purchasing agent was a man of principle, and he decided that he didn't want to do business with anyone who wouldn't admit shortcomings.

II. Ben Hawkes was selling his fiber glass cabin cruiser. He was selling it after the season, so he knew that he would not get top dollar, but his children had grown up and moved away and he didn't want the responsibility of owning a large boat that he would have to work on alone.

It was clearly a buyer's market for boats, and for the first two weeks Ben didn't even get a nibble. Finally a shrewd old man came aboard to see the boat. He looked unimpressed at the features Ben showed him. He looked positively crestfallen when he listened to the engines idling. Then he made Ben an offer of about 50% of what he was asking. "It's a little on the low side, but then there are mighty big expenses here. Winter's coming and I have to pull her out and work on those engines. Of course you can keep up the payments and sell her in the spring; you might do a little better." The old fellow's psychology worked and Ben, fearful of losing his only prospect accepted the ridiculous offer. Actually he would have been better off standing pat. If he calculated the money it would take to carry and maintain the boat over the winter it would have been only a small part of the price he could have realized had he sold the boat when the market turned to favor the sellers. But he was impatient, and he paid for it. In effect he negotiated himself a handsome loss!

EXAMPLES OF INDIVIDUALS WHO USED THEIR OUT SUCCESSFULLY

Harry Ames was a young fellow with a small printing plant which was is located in the financial center of a large city. Harry was the foreman, but he was also the salesman going out with regularity to try to drum up business. One day he was having lunch at a local restaurant, and he struck up a conversation with an amiable fellow who told him that he was a purchasing agent for a large chartering firm. This man bought a great volume of business forms, and Harry asked if he could bid on the work. He was literally dancing for joy when his "new friend" called him back and said that he liked his bid and that he would like to send some business his way. Harry cooled off considerably when his friend mentioned that the only hitch was that he wasn't going to pay in thirty days as Harry's estimate sheet indicated. He was presently enjoying ninety days from his printer and that would have to remain. He reminded Harry of the volume of work he was promising and rang off.

Harry was in a deep quandary. The volume of work from this one account would mean almost 40% increase in his overall business. That would be a tremendous increase. He could buy more modern equipment and increase his staff. But he kept looking at his ledgers, and he knew that there was no way that he could extend this much credit for ninety days— in fact it might even be longer; bills always take longer rather than sooner to be paid, and the customer was starting off *asking* for ninety days! In the end Harry called back his friend and told him that he was sorry, but that he just couldn't handle that much credit. He could save the man money, but he needed to be paid in thirty days net.

As it turned out Harry did the wise thing. This purchasing agent was an old fox who knew that small printers of Harry's size were continually going in and out of business. The longer he held them up for their money the better the chance of not having to pay the bill at all if they went out of business. He was doing the same thing with three or four other small printers, and it was only Harry's integrity and his ability to get out of the negotiations that saved him a loss that could have been devastating.

Summary:

- Every mature-minded businessman must learn to make a virtue of necessity. Some negotiations just were not meant to be, and it is best to accept that and go on to more productive interests.

- If something doesn't feel right—it probably isn't. Unless you can live with your settlement, you shouldn't make it.

- It is certainly true that half a loaf is better than none—but there are times when no loaf is even better than half!

- Many times the negotiator wins by losing—in the long run.

You can plan so that the amicable agree-
... will allow you to draw on your trite
... count...

11.

· The Piggyback Technique

Objectives:

- To define and describe the negotiating technique called "piggybacking"

- To illustrate the technique by example and to
emphasize the importance of using it as part of
most negotiations

- To explain the application of this technique in
all its variations to negotiating and business

The "piggyback" technique is a method that is
best used in the middle of negotiations. It involves
using the solution of one negotiating point to win
another point.

For example, if a labor union is negotiating with
management for increased benefits and wages, it
might be to management's benefit to come forward
and make a quick concession on benefits and piggyback off that agreement to demand a quick response from the union on the wage increases. The

theory is that agreement is contagious and that agreement on one point will bring the parties closer together on another.

The successful use of this method requires careful thinking about what is really the priority item in your negotiations. Then by carefully structuring the negotiations you can plan so that the amicable agreement of point A will allow you to close on your true objective, point B.

TWO CASE HISTORIES OF PIGGYBACKING

I: Joe James was an antique collector. Like most antique collectors he was not completely rational when it came to his favorite hobby. There was a 17th century doll house that he found in a small antique shop in an outlying region of the country. It was filled with small antique model furniture and other carvings that the proprietess had labeled "not for sale." The price of the doll house was $800. Joe offered the lady $1,600 for the completely furnished doll house. She refused, saying that the furnishings had a special place in her heart and she couldn't afford to part with them. She even pointed out that strictly from a historical point of view they didn't even really fit into this doll house. Joe listened carefully. He knew now that the woman really didn't have any strong feelings about the doll house but that is the item that he wanted. So he reluctantly agreed to take the doll house alone. This made the woman feel happier. They settled on the price of $650. Had Joe not made a point of asking for the furnishings, there would have been no settlement, and the woman might not have been so anxious to drop her price.

II: One of the most frequent users of the piggyback technique is a good salesman. J.D. Hoover, a representative of a company that manufactures electric typewriters and other office equipment, piggybacks all the time when he makes his sales presentations. "Tell me, Mr. Manager, how much does it cost each time your company sends out a personal letter?" If the manager doesn't know, J.D. does; he presents a survey done by a research firm that shows that the average letter costs a company $5! The rendering of a simple invoice costs $10! "And that," he says "is if you have a crackerjack operator at the keyboard." "Otherwise," he says somberly, "it could cost even more. Now I ask you, Mr. Manager, wouldn't you like to know how you could reduce this cost and at the same time reduce the errors in any of your company correspondence?" The manager has to say *yes*. "Would you agree that if my machine reduced your cost of a letter by $1 that according to this price it would pay for itself within six months time?" Again, the manager says *yes*. The next step is for the manager to okay a demonstration of the machine. After getting into the habit of saying *yes*, he is easily piggybacked by the persuasive salesman into an excellent buying position.

WIDER APPLICATIONS OF THE PIGGYBACK TECHNIQUE

The piggyback technique can also have a much wider application. This usually happens when the user takes advantage of the fact of known success and then piggybacks this historical fact to his own advantage. The user of the technique then aligns himself with the success and thus gains leverage by the association. At the very simplest level, let's take the example of an employee who wants to ask for new responsibilities by piggybacking off the success of a predecessor. "You see, sir, this is no more than what Bob Walker did so well a few years back. The only difference is that the forms I design will be a little simpler to reflect the new power of the machine language we are now using." Providing that old Bob Walker did make a name for himself, the supervisor would be hard-pressed to find an objection to the request.

PIGGYBACKING FROM A DISTANCE

You can also piggyback on the techniques of another company. "Mr. Supervisor, did you notice today's *Wall Street Journal?* There is a detailed article about how United has been experimenting with unbundling some of their customer services. I had an idea along those lines that I would like to discuss with you." Here the negotiator gains instant credibility by aligning his idea with a similar idea already implemented by a large corporation in the same field.

The effectiveness of the piggyback approach is obvious. It is also one of the most potent techniques available to the negotiator. One of the most powerful forces in business is "what came before." People feel comfortable with the way things are, and they like to be able to detect familiar trends in new developments. Behind every major scam and swindle in the history of American finance is a con man who got his way by creating the illusion that he was working under standard operating procedures. The force of the status quo is a powerful force indeed.

PIGGYBACK TECHNIQUE AS FOREGONE CONCLUSION

The piggyback technique can be used with extra effect if the presentation of the technique is embellished with a lavish amount of enthusiasm. "Mr. Client, this report shows what our software did for the Lemmas Corporation—and they didn't have anywhere near the market penetration that you do. The only reservation I have about using our procedures with you is that the Justice Department will stop us because it is unfair to the competition."

PIGGYBACK FROM COMMON EXPERIENCE

In this application the user of the technique has some common ground with the adversary and uses that common ground to piggyback to a substantive point. "Mr. James, I really do feel for your position because I was there myself. I once operated a small business, and I was forever ducking phone calls from creditors. I *know* that you want to make your payments, but sometimes the money just isn't there, and you have to make the best of it. Any reasonable person in business knows that. But on the other hand, Mr. James, your credibility and your credit are also important to your success. So why don't you and I try to work out some kind of token payment just to show good faith to the front office? I'm sure that if they see you're trying, they won't want to pressure you too much."

PIGGYBACK TECHNIQUE IN ADVERTISING

If a franchise advertised itself as the "MacDonald's

of the 1980s" the line would undoubtedly create a lot of interest. Why? Because the name of a known success instantly communicates with the public. No words are wasted; the message is conveyed instantly, and the very association with a major success story lends a certain amount of credibility to the company making the claim.

This is the reason why patent attorneys are kept busy protecting trademarks, tradenames and slogans. It also goes back to that tried and true negotiating technique—the piggyback approach.

THE PIGGYBACK APPROACH IN REVERSE

By making reference to a notable flop and indicating how your approach is different, you can suddenly seem like a very smart fellow indeed. This is the approach used by many stockbrokers who prospect for accounts among investors who have lost money with previous brokers. It isn't difficult to be a genius in hindsight and to criticize the offending brokers soundly for being imprudent and silly. In the light of devastation even the merest hint of reason is enough to win an investor's trust.

ONE NOTE OF CAUTION

One note of caution for the piggyback approach: don't use it too many times in the same negotiating session. If you do, your talk will take on the sound of a university lecture, and your adversary may very well yawn and lose interest in the conversation. Be selective on the points that you piggyback and push them for all they are worth.

Summary:

- The basis of the piggyback technique is that agreement on one point is contagious and leads to agreement on other points.

- The skillful negotiator assigns priority to his goals and reaches agreement on a less important point in order to piggyback to success on issues that are more important to him.

12.
Keeping It Simple

Objectives:

- To make the point that clarity and clear thinking are a virtue

- To show that negotiations are communication and that communication must be clear and unambiguous

- To present a case history illustrating a clearly presented negotiation

We have spoken before about the importance of clear communication in negotiations. In fact, a negotiation, in its highest form, is an advanced state of communication. It does seem to be true that the successful negotiator is a person who is an expert at clarifying and conveying a point of view to an adversary.

So no matter what your personality or negotiating tactics, your success will depend on your ability to "get across" to your opponent.

The best way that we know to accomplish this is to move your discussions carefully, point by point, without attempting to cover too much at one time.

The best analogy that we have heard to describe the importance of this aspect of the art is to compare negotiating with eating a good steak dinner. The way to get maximum enjoyment and maximum benefit from the steak is to: 1. cut small, easy-to-handle pieces; 2. chew each piece carefully; 3. swallow; and 4. digest. If you follow these same four steps with your negotiations you will be on the road to success.

The reasoning isn't hard to follow. Communication is difficult. Clarity will not come about by itself. It is *your* job to create order out of chaos. The easiest way to do this is to proceed point by point. If you look around you, you will see that the most effective advertising copy is not the cleverest but the simplest. The most successful writers use the words that are easiest to understand. This doesn't happen by accident. To present an argument simply does not mean that *you* are simple. It does mean that you have that argument clearly in mind and that you can express it effectively. The people who don't have a clear vision of what they want are the people who find it impossible to cut their steak into bite-size pieces. These are the people who cut off pieces that are too large and end up choking on their dinner.

THE VIRTUES OF SIMPLICITY

Never be afraid of offending anyone with simplicity. It will not happen. Somehow people have the idea that practitioners in any field of interest will be bored by reading about that field in simple, easy to understand terms. But this isn't the case. It is true that much writing of the corporate and even academic nature is overly technical and filled with jargon but this is not because the people who are going to be reading it *want* it this way. It is always easier to do something poorly than it is to do something well. It is easier to write using half images which approximate what you want to say than it is to take the time to say it precisely. But if you do take that time, your audience will be appreciative.

So the first step is to break up your discussion into compact and understandable little bites of information and begin to "chew" on them with your adversary.

The next step is to let your adversary swallow and digest, but don't take too much of this activity on faith. Make reference to points that you have communicated and return to them. Think of our friend the cow which has four stomachs to make sure that its cud is thoroughly digested. Don't be afraid to return to key points and exhibit a little redundancy. It's an effective method and, again, it will not be resented. Indeed, studies have shown that most individuals actually enjoy using information that they have just learned.

Think of yourself as a chef serving a grand meal or as a maestro conducting a symphony orchestra. Become master to the conversation by the way that you introduce and dismiss point by point as you move toward your goal. Don't think that this is easy. Even people who are "naturally persuasive" will have difficulty breaking down what they do into parts. In fact many times experts at certain techniques are at a complete loss about how to teach their technique to others. But make no mistake, it is a learnable technique and, like a sunrise, or the flight of a bird, it can be dissected for study.

CASE HISTORY IN SIMPLICITY

Recently we taped a session with a fellow who is a most effective negotiator, and we have taken the liberty of dissecting his approach for your information.

The session took place in the chamber of a wily lawyer representing the real estate holdings of a large estate. The lawyer is negotiating with a well-known real estate broker who has earned his reputation by "assembling" entire blocks of real estate for large developers. Assemblage is a complicated skill involving discretion and the ability to negotiate on your feet. There aren't too many good assemblers around; this fellow was one of the best. The object of their talks was a small townhouse owned by the estate in an area of town that is ready for quick development. There is a problem with the house. It should have been sold off years ago because its location is worth far more than its residential value. However, an eccentric brother and sister team lived there for years and refused to sell. They had now met their final reward, and the house was being rented on a month-to-month basis until the estate could decide what to do with the property.

For the sake of the conversation, let's assume that a fair market value for the property is $250,000. Let's pick up our study with the real estate broker who begins the session.

"Hello again, Mr. X, I'm glad to see you. As I told you on the phone I have a client who is definitely interested in 345 (the address of the house in point), and I wanted to come by in person to present this offer to you."

"Very well, Mr. Y. As you may know, an estate owns that property so that any offer I receive must be turned over to them in writing, and then they will meet and decide. That's a valuable piece of real estate for the right person."

"Yes, my client thinks so too, but of course he is interested only in the land under the house."

"Quite naturally, but you know, Mr. Y, I get calls all the time about that house. And quite naturally I keep the executors of the estate advised of all interest. Just last week I had an offer that fell short."

"Well, you know, Mr. X, that an offer is not something you can put in a museum. Things change quickly, and you and I both know that timing is everything. Now you don't think I would take up my valuable time and yours unless there was serious interest on my client's part?"

"Yes of course, Mr. Y. By the way," he said this picking up a pen in a very official manner, "who is your client?"

"Quite naturally, Mr. X, my client prefers to remain in the background for now." (He said this with no change in facial expression.) "He feels that since he is rather well known, the information that he is in the market for 345 will not be to his advantage."

"Yes, quite understandable, well, let's get on with it. What is the offer?"

The two men had been seated. Now the real estate broker rose to his full height and began walking toward his adversary as if he were delivering the crown jewels. "I have been authorized to offer you in the name of my client, the sum of $175,000 in cash for 345. This offer will stand for exactly ten days, which should give you all the time that you need to talk to your people." At the conclusion of these words the broker was standing above the lawyer looking down at him and clearly pressuring him to make the next move and make it good.

"Ha, ha, $175,000. Well out of respect to you, Mr. Y, I will pass along this bid, but I can only inform you that only last week they passed up a much more generous offer."

"As I said," said the broker (returning to his point), "timing is always a consideration. And add on the fact that this offer is coming from a man who can simply write you a check with no banks or boards of directors to hold things up. Surely it is worth something to be so close to the man who is writing the check."

"As I said, Mr. Y, I will pass this along. Will you now please put your bid in writing on your stationery so that I may make my presentation."

"I am sorry, sir, I cannot do that."

"But isn't your bid bona fide?" asked the attorney with irony.

"Yes it is, but I have been burnt this way too often. Once your people have a written bid, they can use that to squeeze whoever is bidding against me. I'm sorry, Mr. X, but you'll have to depend upon my word and my reputation in the field. I cannot in good conscience reduce anything to writing."

You will notice the clear crisp manner in which this negotiation moved forward. Even though nothing eventually came of the meeting, the bid was too low, and as you might have guessed from the proceedings, the "buyer" represented by the broker was none other than the broker himself. But even so, it is instructive to see how two experienced adversaries feel each other out and engage each other with good humor and friendship even while each knows the other's game. And indeed, it could have worked. If the taxes on the property were coming due or if the estate needed money for lawyers' fees or other expenses, Mr. Y might well have bought himself a real bargain.

Negotiation is after all communication. You don't negotiate to impress your adversary (although it doesn't hurt to do this); you negotiate to express. And even though Mr. Y didn't buy himself a bargain, he did express his feelings about the property in no uncertain terms.

Summary:

- Negotiation is communication. Therefore, real negotiations depend on clarity and brevity of thought.

- In the end, clear thinking and effective presentation will win more negotiating points than any kind of obfuscation.

13.

Learning to Listen

Objectives:

- To stress the importance of learning to be a good listener as part and parcel of being a good negotiator

- To offer a list of precise points that will help the reader develop listening skills

LEARNING TO LISTEN THE NEGOTIATING WAY

Communication is not simply talking and listening in turn. In order for communication to take place, information has to be conveyed between the two negotiators. Clearly one half ot this bargain is for the case you present to be simple, well thought out and logical. The other half of communication is conveying this information to your adversary. To do this you will have to listen. Only by listening can you learn to understand the other person and determine how best to communicate.

Learning to be a good listener is an important negotiating skill for two reasons. First of all, listening will key you into the person you are addressing; it will enable you to latch on to what is important to this person and to communicate with him. Second, it can be devastating to negotiations if one party thinks that he is *not* being listened to. Any parent or teacher knows instantly the tremendous frustration that comes of talking and not being listened to.

Think of your conversation as a tennis match; not as a session on a golf driving range. In the first case two players are involved and both of them are interacting. In the second example two individuals are shooting for the long ball and one simply waits his turn while the other plays. This latter example is to be avoided at all costs.

To help you improve your listening skills we have put together the following checklist for your information:

- Minimize Talk: It is axiomatic that you can't listen while you are talking—an obvious point that nevertheless never occurs to many people.

- Relate: Try to understand (standunder) your adversary. Attempt to see things through his or her eyes. This is one of the most important ways to improve your listening skills.

- Show Interest: There is no better way to convince your adversary that you have been listening than to ask questions or request clarification of the topics he is discussing.

- Recapitulate Discussions: Cover key parts. This is an effective communication method. Do it factually, however, without editorializing or making any judgments.

- Communicate: Express not to impress.

- Strive To Be Understanding: Remember the word *K.I.S.S.—Keep It Simple Stupid*. Use simple, common words.

- Analyze The Other Person: Study the face, mouth and eyes of your adversary. Pinpoint your attention to the adversary's physical presence. This will help you listen and, at the same time, absolutely convince the adversary that you are listening.

- Zero In: Try to focus on the main point of your adversary's conversation. Make a studied effort to look past anecdotes, stories and statistics and settle on the essence of what is being said.

- Don't Argue Mentally: The fact that you and your opponent are adversaries means that there will be any number of points about which you will disagree. However, to interrupt his discourse, even mentally, will be to set up a barrier to communication. Learn to control yourself and curb your desire to fight. Relax and make note of the points for later discussion.

- Don't Make Assumptions: Assumptions will almost always lead you away from your true objective. Therefore you should make a real effort (it won't be easy) to avoid assumptions about your adversary. Don't assume, for example, that your adversary uses terms the same way you do; don't assume that he is trying to embarrass you by eye contact or facial expression. Sometimes assumptions can be correct, but it is best to avoid them if you possibly can as they are more often than not barriers to effective communication.

- Don't Make Hasty Judgments: It's too easy to judge in any case. Therefore give your opponent the benefit of the doubt by reserving judgment—at least until the facts are in.

- Watch Out For Your Own Prejudice: Even the most liberal-minded of us harbor certain prejudices. It is worth your while to be as honest concerning your own prejudices as you can and allow for these prejudgments when you are trying to listen to your adversary's case.

- Take Notes: An aid to listening that will have an effect of focusing your attention on what is said and in flattering your adversary is note taking. Wouldn't you be flattered if someone thought enough of what you had to say to write it down?

- Translate Into Your Own Words and Verify With Your Adversary: To avoid any later misunderstanding it is best to put key gains into your own terms and then to ask for verification in those terms. Only by this verbal cross-pollination can you really communicate precisely.

In addition to the above list there are certain verbal cues that tell you that something is up. We have mentioned only a few but actually many of them are dropped during a typical negotiating session. Watch for anything that jars against the normal flow of the conversation, anything that causes nervousness or stiffness in the adversary or anything said that doesn't seem to get any feedback at all.

Here are a few of our favorite examples:

By the way . . . A person saying "by the way" means to imply that something has just popped into his mind, and he wants to tell you about it before he forgets. The implication is that the point is unimportant. Actually people using this term are really saying that the point in question is quite important to them. Listen to it well.

Frankly . . . This is a strange one. Logically, points prefaced by "frankly" imply that the adversary is not being frank or honest about other points. What a person is really saying by his use of this term is "I really want you to pay close attention to what I am about to say because I think it is important." It has nothing to do with frankness or honesty necessarily but it is a cue that your adversary is about to say something important and worth concentrating upon.

Before I forget . . . This is similar to "by the way." It is a cloaking of a point very important to the adversary in terms that render it superficially unimportant. It is a rather silly phrase when you think about it but it is frequently used and should signal you that something important to the negotiations is about to be mentioned.

This list is deceptively simple. But don't just read over it and go on. Think about each point and consider how you can use it in your negotiations; once you become a good listener you will find that people will want to talk to you and you will learn more and gain prestige in their eyes.

Summary:

- A negotiator who knows how to listen will be an efficient and productive negotiator.

- A good listener is keyed to the adversary's personality and needs and knows how to react to them. A good listener is more able to control the flow of negotiations and to place his points more effectively than the negotiator who doesn't listen but only waits for his turn to speak.

14.
The "Walk Away" Technique

Objectives:

- To define and describe the process of abruptly halting and restarting a negotiating session that is not going well

- To explain the benefits and the positive input that come from using the "walk away" technique

WALKING AWAY: PUTTING NEGOTIATIONS TO THE TEST!

The "walk away" is a method that is used in the middle of negotiations when the action is stalled. When executed correctly it has the effect of clearing the air and allowing pressure to escape so that a new start can be made.

Another important feature of the "walk away" is the element of surprise that can be an effective escape route for you if your opponent has been getting the better of you or if you don't feel comfortable with the way the negotiation is progressing. It is similar to the clinch in boxing which allows one fighter to hold the action while he gets his bearings back.

EXECUTING THE "WALK AWAY"

Assume that you are in a negotiating session and you notice to your dismay that you are hearing the same arguments and counter-arguments over and over again. The talks are not getting anyplace and neither is the current method of moving the talks. As soon as one of you mentions an alternative point there is not enough momentum to leave the present point of contention and go on to more promising areas. Therefore you decide to take matters into your own hands. You get up and announce to your adversary, "Look, I think that maybe the two of us are trying too hard, and that's probably the reason that we aren't getting anyplace. I suggest that we break it here and come back in an hour." Then, before your adversary has a chance to consider your proposal, you turn and walk away.

THE BENEFIT OF THE "WALK AWAY"

Two main results are due to your actions. First of all the air is cleared and the contention of the discussion has been dissipated. In addition, by taking the initiative and walking out you have left your adversary in a position where he must become introspective. In most cases this will work to your advantage as it will cause your adversary to consider what *he* said or did to make you leave.

When you return, try to take a new approach or settle on another area so that you avoid the previous stalemate. Although sometimes it is perfectly all right to return to the exact bone of contention that set you walking in the first place.

This is the same technique you see used by a baseball batter who grows weary of the mind-games being played by the pitcher. If the pitcher is trying to psych him by using delaying tactics, the astute batter will play the same game and step out of the batter's box. Often the only thing he will do is stretch, but it's the breaking of the routine that's important. If the pitcher has been building up tension he has lost his advantage because the batter, by simply stepping away, has changed the game plan. You can do the same thing effectively in your negotiating sessions.

Please realize that walking away is *not* a sign of defeat or even a sign of discouragement. It is actually a positive approach to a situation that is beginning to turn negative. All you are doing by walking out on a session is to restate symbolically to your adversary that you want the negotiations to succeed and you are willing to try as many approaches as necessary to accomplish this success.

Summary:

- There is no rule to negotiations that says you must finish what you start without interruption.

- When negotiations are not proceeding well there is a simple and effective remedy. Break the negotiations and come back fresh. The pause will be good for you and thought provoking for your adversary.

15.

Reading the Opposition: A Negotiator's Guide to Body Language

Objectives:

- To make the point that important cues are sometimes communicated without spoken words

- To discuss several key examples of body language that occur with frequency in negotiation and to present reasonable counters to them

Negotiations are communications. But all communication is not necessarily verbal. Indeed, a look, a gesture, or an attitude can tell you more than words can.

For this reason it is worth your while to consider the ways in which your adversary's body is telegraphing information that can help you to success in your negotiations.

THE PIPE SMOKER

The pipe smoker generally uses his pipe as a crutch or security blanket in negotiations. The trick with this type of adversary is not to compete with the pipe for the smoker's attention. For example, when the smoker reaches for a match to light his pipe, this is your cue to stop talking. Wait until he has lighted up and is puffing before you continue with the conversation. In the best possible cases the pipe is a distraction, and it will be to your advantage to take your adversary's security blanket away tactfully. The easiest way is to watch the pipe. All pipes go out eventually and have to be put in an ashtray or piperack temporarily. Before the impulse to take up the pipe returns, hand your adversary something. Give him a page of figures, a brochure or anything that will involve him in your conversation.

EYEGLASS CLEANERS

The moment your adversary removes his eyeglasses and begins to clean them, this is your cue to pause. Why? Eyeglass cleaning is a signal that the cleaner is carefully considering a point. Therefore when this happens, don't press, allow your adversary the necessary room to consider and then gently take up the negotiations when the glasses are back in position.

THE LAID-BACK ADVERSARY

Some people are very relaxed and laid-back. Instead of sitting up straight and alert, these people might slouch or even put up their feet. There is nothing wrong with being relaxed except that it can interfere with negotiations if the lines of communication are too loose. A good way to tighten them up with a relaxed adversary is through the use of eye contact. Before you move on to the next segment of your talks, make sure that you have your adversary agreeing or disagreeing while making contact. No matter how relaxed he is, it is a rare bird indeed who will not respond to eye contact.

THE NERVOUS NELLY

There are some people who are terrified in any kind of head-to-head negotiations. Their nervousness will be evident. They will look ill at ease and carry their bodies very stiffly. Their conversation will be very tight and not at all spontaneous. All you can do in such a case is to try to loosen up your adversary by making him feel at home. Very often this nervousness occurs in people without an extensive business background. They are in a foreign area and they don't know what to expect. Do not patronize a nervous adversary but simply try to talk directly and thus alleviate the fear that something out of the ordinary is going to happen. You can help your case by suggesting a more comfortable seating arrangement. Or you might take the initiative and loosen *your* tie and roll up your sleeves to show that things are going to be relaxed and comfortable.

Some people are so nervous that they can make *you* nervous if you are not careful. Don't let this happen. Remember that nobody wants to be nervous. Everyone wants to feel good and be comfortable. Therefore if you set aside your adversary's nervousness, he will feel better, be grateful to you and this will aid your negotiations.

KNEE SHAKERS

Dealing with a knee shaker is frustrating but it has the advantage of setting your immediate goal clearly in front of you: you have to get the knee to stop shaking. If you don't, no progress will be made. The way to stop a knee shaker from shaking is very obvious: get him up on his feet. Knee shaking is one nervous habit that you can't perform while standing up. So your job is simply to get your adversary out of the chair and up on his feet. Go to lunch, go for a drink or better yet suggest a nice brisk walk. Because you know now that your adversary gets very nervous when he is sitting, you should make an attempt to close the deal while walking. By the way, this is a method that was used with great success by former Secretary of State Henry Kissinger, who was a great advocate of this "walking negotiations" theory.

BE INTUITIVE

Somehow the idea has developed that people need to have a public face in business and a private face that they take home at night. While it is certainly true that you are going to be different in an attorney's office, for example, than you would be in your own bedroom, it is worth remembering that you don't stop being a human being no matter what your location. You should not stop trusting your basic instincts whether you are dealing with a business or a personal negotiation.

There is nothing magical about intuition. All it

really means is that the intuitive person has a great amount of patience for details of observation and for nuances of behavior.

Take an interest in your adversary. Pay attention to the way he is acting and perk up if something seems to be wrong. Oftentimes a hesitancy, impatience or crossness will be the direct result of the issues that you are negotiating. If this is the case then react to this barrier and try to make your point from another direction. But your adversary could be reacting to something else. It might be the way that you are making a point. If you have a very strong personality it might be that your adversary is not comfortable and therefore is becoming ultrasensitive about *all* the issues being discussed.

Be watchful of coughing, finger drumming, pencil twirling and other signs of impatience or nervousness. They will have to be dealt with before you can get the negotiations moving.

In short, while it is best to *act* relaxed in any negotiating session, you cannot really *be* relaxed. You should be working every minute that you are there, observing your adversary and continuously thinking of ways to influence him to your way of thinking. Whether your adversary tells you something in words or by the way he twiddles his moustache, you must react to this information in a way that will result in real communication.

Summary:

- The human voice is the primary negotiating instrument; however the skilled negotiator can learn to receive valuable cues from non-verbal communication as well.

- Learning to evaluate non-verbal cues is a valuable skill because often the adversary is actually unaware of what his body is telling you. Perception, therefore, can give you a definite competitive edge.

16.

Five Flags That Signal Success

Objective:

- To identify and explain five key signs that the negotiations are turning in your direction and will soon be successfully concluded!

There are some easily identifiable signs that the tides of negotiations have turned in your direction. Early identification of these signs is an important asset as it will allow you to reinforce your strong points and reach a quicker and stronger final agreement.

It is also valuable to know that you are winning because it is a signal for you to be gracious and also to moderate your approach to avoid overkill.

Basically, the signs that signal your imminent success are:

- Counter agreements are reduced. At this point in the negotiations there are fewer points of contention and more discussion of points in which you are in accord. You will be able to detect your adversary's genuine desire to work to an agreeable conclusion.

- Your and your adversary's points are closer together.

- Your adversary asks about final arrangements. This is the point that really tells you that you are getting close. It is as any experienced real estate broker will tell you. "When the buyer asks about the roof, it is about time to write up the sale!"

- Adversary extends personal invitation to you and your spouse. This is something that is not going to happen unless it is clear that you and your adversary will do business. Once you receive such an invitation closing the deal is a matter only of formality.

- Willingness to put your agreement in writing. If an adversary is sincere, he will have no objection to putting the deal in writing. If such a willingness exists, do not delay. Get out any kind of paper and any kind of writing instrument and draw up a quick written agreement. It might seem silly to seal a deal on the back of an envelope or on a paper napkin, but it is a good preliminary to final formalization. Again, if your adversary is dealing in good faith there should be no objection to putting it in writing. The understanding, of course, is that a formal agreement will be drawn up and presented to the adversary for signature.

A final point about this. When the formal agreement has been drawn up, either by you or your attorney or both, do *not* put it in the mail. You have shown commitment by your diligence in the negotiations and now you should prove commitment by meeting personally over the formal agreement for the added formality of signing. In addition to adding an element of importance to the transaction, it will help you cement the negotiations that you have just completed.

Summary:

- Knowing that you are reading your negotiating goals will allow you to moderate your approach and thus bring the negotiations to a gracious and friendly close.

17.

The Finishing Touches

Objectives:

- To learn to be a good winner
- To understand the importance of cementing negotiations

There is much sanctimonious talk in our society about being a good loser. We stress winning but we teach our kids not to be "sore losers" or "spoilsports." Actually this view is out of line for the business person. We tend to think of winning and losing in such definite terms. Like winning an election or winning the Super Bowl. Actually life and business are a series of successes and failures and if we win one day, chances are that we may not win the next and vice versa.

For this reason it is not enough to be a "good loser." It is equally as important to be a "good winner."

If you prevail in a negotiating session, NEVER

gloat or hold it over your adversary. Even if he tried to backstab you and you turned the tables, do not allow yourself the luxury of joyous revenge. Why? Because you are in the game for the long run. Every step you take is part of a longer career, and the only way to have a really successful career in any field is to enjoy the respect and admiration of the people with whom you are dealing.

As we stated before, it is not a good idea to use the win-lose metaphor in negotiations. If an agreement is made both sides actually win. Having a winner and a loser necessitates bad feelings and envy, and overall produces a very negative situation. Negative energy is the force that you most want to avoid.

CEMENTING YOUR NEGOTIATIONS

After you complete your negotiations you will want to be gracious and understanding and you will definitely want to cement the negotiations that you have just completed.

Send your adversary a letter thanking him for the opportunity of doing business. Mention in clear terms that you are looking forward to a long working relationship and include some praise for the kind of person your adversary is and how much you enjoyed dealing with him.

The next step in cementing your relationships is to send your adversary a gift. Decide on a gift by using the same skills that you used in the research segment of your negotiations. Think about your adversary; think about the way his office was furnished. Think about the kind of person he is. Then select a gift that will fill these three criteria. 1. It must be something that conforms with your adversary's interests and self-image. 2. It must be expensive. 3. It should be something that he will have to display as something for his desk or wall. That way he will *have* to think of you when he looks at it.

The reason it should be expensive is that it has to make a positive impression *and* it must be valuable enough so that he wouldn't think of giving it away or putting it away.

A friend of ours, a young lady who lives in a high-rent district of town, once confided that she was astonished at the number of gift shops that were crowded onto her little street. She couldn't understand how there could be so much demand for expensive, exotic gifts. The answer, of course, is that most of these gifts were purchased to celebrate a successful negotiation. And as long as capitalism and free enterprise prevail, the gift shop proprietors will continue to do a boom business.

Summary:

- You are in the business world or professional world for the long run. Therefore it is important that along with winning the minor battles you also build a reputation as a fair and honest negotiator.

- The way that you finish up your negotiating sessions will probably be the way that your adversary remembers you. Therefore be gracious and courteous and retain the respect of your adversary along with the benefits of a successful negotiation.

18.

Negotiating to Buy Your Own Business

Objectives:

- How to look "behind" the numbers to negotiate a better deal

- How to diagnose "people" problems, and to determine if they will make or break a deal

In this chapter we are going to discuss the place of negotiations in buying your own business. We will limit our discussion to existing businesses that you can buy, namely a franchise business or a going business that is owned and operated by an independent business person. We will also talk briefly about the role of negotiations in starting a new business from scratch.

In this case it goes without saying that the prospective buyer should enlist as much expert advice as possible before making a decision.

NEGOTIATING TO BUY A FRANCHISE BUSINESS

The greatest advantage of choosing a franchised business over an independent opportunity is the "head start" that you inherit by opening your doors as part of a larger going concern. This track record of the franchisor pays dividends in helping you to learn the business quickly, helping you to run your business smoothly and, most importantly, helping you to get business more easily.

Recently the franchise concept got a tremendous boost when an old established restaurant chain in a major U.S. city decided to convert the bulk of its locations into outlets of one of the larger and better known hamburger franchises. The old chain was not doing well and felt that a switch to fast foods was its salvation. Why didn't the chain simply offer a fast food menu and open its doors? The president of the firm explained that he had considered doing that. After all, the chain had a number of years in the business and could cook hamburgers as well as anybody. But it did its own studies and found that the sales of a little known and new fast food restaurant could be as much as 45% less in the same location than if customers were offered the familiar fare of one of the fast food giants. The old restaurant chain made its conversion and has never looked back since. This is one of the best examples of the benefits of the franchise system.

Of course, it isn't all advantages. Franchise regulations are usually stringent, and certain expenses, such as local advertising, are often mandated by the franchise agreement. Of course each year a percentage of each franchisee's sales must be paid in the form of a fee to the franchisor. Still, this fee can be regarded as a small price to pay if the franchise is successful.

Another advantage is that because of the popularity of franchising, there are ever-growing numbers of different kinds of businesses that you can get into via the franchise method. A handy listing of the choices is offered by a publication entitled *Franchise Opportunities Handbook,* published by the U.S. Department of Commerce.

This variety increases the chances that you will be able to select a franchise business in a field that appeals to you and in which you have interest and aptitude.

SELECTING A FRANCHISE BUSINESS

The key difference between a franchise business and an independent business lies in the back up that the new franchisee will receive from the parent organization. The decision about whether you are suited to a certain kind of business is entirely up to you and doesn't really have anything to do with how the business is organized. If you wouldn't be happy in the restaurant business, it really wouldn't matter if you were operating a slick franchise or a very unique and independent cafe. That's why the first thing that you should do is think about the kind of business that would make you happy. Don't depend solely on your feelings to come to this decision. If you are considering buying a business, you are talking about a considerable investment. To safeguard that investment you are going to have to do some homework. Get out and talk to other people in the same kind of business. Determine if you have anything in common with these people. Do the things that make them happy make you happy? Go to the library and read all you can about the industry you are considering. Pay special attention to the trade magazines as they are an excellent source of information on the current state of the industry and its problems both present and future. If possible, try to get a job in the industry that you are considering; this tactic will give you another view of the business and will teach you quickly whether it is a business that you want to be in.

Once you decide on the type of business you want, the next step is to review your capital resources and to make a list of the franchises in your field that you can afford. When you have done that you are ready to begin making your choice. Contact each company and gather as much preliminary information as you can. Become familiar with all their terms, both industry and financial, that you will be encountering. From here on it is a matter of sitting down with the people close to you—your spouse and family, and also with your lawyers and accountant and possibly (we recommend it) with a business consultant—to determine which franchise opportunity is the best one for you. This is not a simple decision and will depend upon many factors including market saturation, site selection, market potential, profit potential, future prospects, and many other important factors.

For the sake of brevity we will skip to the assumption that you have used your resources to make a prudent decision and are now ready to enter final negotiations with the franchisor.

The next step in the progression is for you to put up your money and sign a franchise agreement. Then you and the franchisor will work together to put you in business. This sounds straightforward enough, but these two little sentences contain a world of possibilities, each of which can be critical to your success in your new business. It is always a good idea to plan ahead in business. In the franchisee-franchisor relationship this means to anticipate the provisions of the franchise agreement and determine how it can be modified to suit your own needs.

DEVELOPING A NEGOTIATING ATTITUDE

Generally speaking, the leverage in the franchisor-franchisee negotiations belongs to the franchisor. In most cases the franchisor is a relatively large company with a track record of success in its field. The franchisee on the other hand is a newcomer, most often wet behind the ears, with very little, if any, experience running his own business. Such an individual is easily misled into thinking that the franchisor is "doing him a favor by agreeing to put him in business!" This isn't the case. Don't be browbeaten or psyched-out by the franchisor. Remember that *he needs you* as much as you need him. The franchisor-franchisee relationship is a two-way street and therefore the prospect for good solid negotiations is promising. The only way for the franchisor to grow and increase his market penetration and profits is through the enlistment of competent enthusiastic people such as yourself. Make no mistake about it. You are an important part of the arrangement, and your desires and goals are worth negotiating. So begin your business career with strength—develop an attitude of self-confidence and start thinking about what the franchisor can do for you!

WHAT IS NEGOTIABLE AND WHAT IS NOT

When we speak about negotiations between the franchisor and the franchisee, we are most often talking about the terms and conditions specified in the franchise agreement. Naturally the specifics of this agreement will differ markedly from industry to industry. We will only attempt an overview here. Specific points of negotiation industry-by-industry can best be isolated by using your attorney, accountant or business consultant.

Let's begin with what is generally *not* subject to negotiation. In most cases a franchisor will not budge on the cost of the franchise. While this is not a hard and fast rule, it is true for the most part. This does not mean that there are no other items to be negotiated. The cost of the franchise is clearly important but if the franchise is being sold by a reputable and well-established franchisor, the cost will probably reflect the true value that is going to change hands. Always keep in mind that in the business world "cheap is cheap." A franchise cost of $50,000 can be cheap if it puts you into a business that returns that much to you in the first year. On the other hand a franchise cost of $500 can be too expensive if the business you enter does not have a chance of making it. The franchise fee, therefore, is an important consideration and while you should do some research as to whether or not it is justified, you shouldn't be discouraged if the franchisor refuses to drop the price.

FINANCING

The first item that you should negotiate is the financial terms of the offering. Even though most franchisors have a boilerplate policy for getting their money, there is often room in this area for considerable leeway.

The best place to start is to sit down with your accountant and work out a preliminary cash-flow projection and profit and loss statement. At the preliminary stage this will serve only as a guideline to you to indicate how long the money that you have will last and what kind of sales you will have to show to meet your obligations. Naturally, if you can arrange to pay for your franchise later, perhaps after a grace period during which time you begin to actually operate your business and gain experience, it might be critical to your success.

If you decide that you want to negotiate softer terms for yourself as part of the franchise agreement, you should definitely have something in mind. You will probably be dealing with the franchisor's counsel or with an authorized representative. Show this person your projections and indicate *strongly* why you feel that favorable terms will greatly increase your chances of success—since your success is also his success you will probably find the franchisor sympathetic (provided that your suggestions are reasonable).

USE YOUR BARGAINING "CHIPS"

Even if you have all the cash you need, you might consider using it to gain another kind of negotiating advantage. For example, assume that you have been planning the purchase of a franchise business for some time. You have the money that you need, but you are concerned about training your employees to the specifications of the company. You have read over the company training package, and you just don't think that the time allotted is going to be enough to make your employees proficient in the franchised operation. In this case you can negotiate for what you want by countering with your strong suit. "Mr. Franchisor, I am not going to ask for special terms on the payout of my franchise cost. I am going to write you a check as soon as I sign on the dotted line—but only on the condition that you assure me that I will get the technical and training backup that I will need to become operational. If we re-adjust that clause, I think that we can get right down to business." Had the franchisee simply paid the money as agreed, he would lose an important negotiating edge. Just because the franchisor asks for something, this doesn't mean that it is going to come to him as a foregone conclusion.

There are other items that can be negotiated as well. Site selection is very important to the ultimate success of a franchised business. This is particularly so if the kind of business is not "self-generating in nature" (i.e. a business in which advertising or the special nature of the business will attract customers regardless of location). It could be that the franchisor has selected a site for you which you do not think is as good as it could be. You voice your discontent to the franchisor and recommend an alternate site. You document your choice by showing a traffic report generated by the local chamber of commerce to dramatize the difference in traffic between the two sites. The franchisor points to the greater amount of the lease on the site that you selected, but you counter with the greater sales which should more than offset the difference. Since your fortunes are ultimately linked together, a meeting of the minds occurs, and you tie up the site that you preferred.

Most franchise agreements include clauses specifying that the franchisor will provide training and services necessary to get the franchisee into business. However, you might be particularly concerned about certain parts of the operation about which you know very little. If this is the case, don't keep your fears a secret. Spell out what you want and put your demands right on the table. For example, assume that you have agreed in principle to buy a franchised business that sells speed-reading courses to the general public. You are worried that you could not handle a slow student with a forceful personality who causes disruptions in the class. You are concerned about the situation because you feel that a lack of credibility in a tense situation like that could lose you customers. Besides, you are not very experienced at thinking on your feet, and you are very nervous about the possibility of something going wrong. You bring up this situation to the company, and they make light of it. It is part of the business they say, and you will soon be an old hand. But it is still important to you, and you insist on more personal service as part of your franchise agreement. You ask to have a seasoned instructor run the first sessions with you. This person should be someone who has had a lot of experience dealing with all situations that can arise in the speed-reading classroom. You want that person there not only to deal with whatever comes up, but to serve as a model for you to learn this aspect of the business.

Clearly a franchisor cannot offer extra services to every franchisee, and indeed it is true that because each franchisee is a different individual they will not all *require* the same extra services. However, if you can clearly state why you think that the inclusion of personalized service will benefit your success, it is a rare franchisor that won't try to meet you at least half-way.

NEGOTIATING THE "GRACE PERIOD"

A grace period can be defined as a period of time during which the franchisee is granted relief from the immediate enforcement of his obligations to the franchisor. It is a period of time during which the franchisee will "get established" in his business. The grace period can be a very important factor to the new franchisee for several reasons. It is inevitable that pressures will build in the initial stages of opening a business, and the grace from either franchisor sales quotas or payment schedules could keep the pressures from building up to an intolerable level. Also, if the franchisee's mind is freed from immediate obligations, he can build a firmer foundation for himself by concentrating his full attention on the details of running his new business. Meeting obligations is certainly a critical part of any business person's responsibilities. However, everybody has to start someplace and there is no doubt that a grace period is a useful advantage for the new franchisee. Generally periods of grace last only 30 to 90 days, and after that the financial pressures will be inevitable. But at least the new business will have a running start.

Most grace periods are granted to give the franchisee relief from sales quotas in franchise businesses where quotas are part of the franchise agreement.

But the concept of a grace period can find application in other areas as well. If you feel that your cash-flow will not be able to sustain you through the critical period of development, you could make a good case to the franchisor to allow you to pay off your franchise cost in a more liberal manner than requested. For example, you might begin with a smaller down payment and pay heftier amounts on a month-by-month basis. Your negotiating point would be that the money would be there to meet unexpected cash-flow problems and would allow you to have the peace of mind to concentrate on running your business and promoting new customers.

THE APPROACH TO TAKE

When you sit across from the franchisor to ask him for liberal terms, it is important that you approach him from the right angle. You can't have the attitude of a customer trying to wangle better terms from a vendor. This approach will usually not work because there is not enough strength in your position. Instead you must approach the franchisor as a colleague working with you to solve a mutual problem. "Mr. Franchisor, look at these figures. Now what would happen to us if we hit a dry spot in the summer season? I think that we could build ourselves some insurance by leveling out those payments. If we don't, I just can't see the reward-risk ratio of this thing. Can you?" Of course there is always the chance that the franchisor will not agree. Then you have the option of taking your business elsewhere as well. Always keep in mind that you are *not* the one on the firing line. You don't have to prove any more to the franchisor than he has to prove to you. You are both testing each other, and therefore it is not asking him too much to modify his policy to accommodate a potential profit center—you!

Who is doing whom a favor?

The above advice applies to 95% of franchise offerings where there is a symbiotic relationship between the franchisor and the franchisee. However, there are exceptions. Some of the more well-known franchises are almost "sure things" and therefore the franchisors can be very choosey about whom they sell franchises to. Of course, their franchises are generally very costly and out of the range of most prospective franchisees. However, the situation of the "favored franchisor" is common enough to warrant a few words of discussion.

In the case of a proven franchise winner, part of the negotiations will be to get accepted by the franchisor. Cynics will tell you that money talks, but in the case of the most successful franchises this just is not so. One of the large fast food franchisors has a rule against absentee management. In a case that came to our attention a wealthy investor placed $250,000 in the bank account of a promising young man who was going to front the purchase for him. To the amazement of both of these men the franchisor turned down the young man because he couldn't document where he got the money. In a case like this there were no real negotiations because the buyer was trying to deceive the franchisor and was clearly in the wrong. However, in other cases the prospective franchisee would have to make a good case for himself by putting his best foot forward. This means preparing a resumé listing all the attributes that could be important to the franchisor. This includes job history, affiliations to the community, education, and other proof of business ethics and stability. Then, of course, there are the financial factors; net worth, credit rating and financial references, which are very valuable. Finally there is the presentation of the candidate's "intangible assets." In this part of the negotiations the prospect should show by his personal appearance and attitude that he is an enthusiastic, bright and competent candidate and that the franchisor could not make a better choice.

In any event the prospective franchisee should always put his best foot forward as his credibility greatly increases his negotiating leverage and enables him to ask for greater franchisor concessions.

NEGOTIATE WITH WHOM?

An especially important factor in negotiating with a franchisor is the person with whom you are negotiating. Is that person duly authorized to back up his promises, or is he just a public relations man who will smile and tell you anything that you want to hear?

While your preliminary contact can be with lower-level employees you should make it clear that when it comes to "talking turkey" you want to do it with an officer of the company who has the clout to stand behind his word. Unless you are granted access to the right man, you will be wasting your time by negotiating. As we said in a previous chapter, commitment is necessary for negotiation to take place and unless your adversary has the power to do something for you he is not really committed to your discussions.

It is important to note that often it is better to have no negotiations at all than to negotiate with the wrong man. Such "non-negotiations" can actually be destructive because they can lead you to heightened or lowered expectations that have no bearing on what is truly possible. If the man you want to see is not available, wait until he is available. If that is not forthcoming, it is probably a good idea to look for another franchise. An ethical franchise operation will have no objections to your dealing in good faith with a person who is duly authorized to back up his promises. If you feel that you're getting the runaround and that a franchisor is not cooperating with you, you are probably right. Remember that you are putting up *your money*, and, you are ready to back up your money with your word; the franchisor should be willing to do the same.

THE PRELUDE TO NEGOTIATIONS— PUTTING THE FRANCHISOR ON NOTICE

Probably the single most important thing that a prospective franchisee can do to gain leverage in negotiations is to put the franchisor on the defensive— right up front! It is important because once you make the first move you can set the tone quickly. If you don't, you are apt to fall into a defensive position yourself because you are playing a game against an adversary who knows it much better than you do.

You needn't be rude or brusque to turn the tables on your adversary. You can accomplish a great deal by simply being direct. Walk in with the attitude: "I want you to show *me* why I should buy a franchise from you." Take the initiative. Be the questioner, and let your adversary supply the answers. Don't be pushy or accusatory. Simply plan the questions that you want to ask and be tenacious about getting the answers that you want.

Among the kind of questions that you might want to ask are:

- How long have you been in business?

- How many franchises are currently being operated?

- How many franchises have been opened last year?

- Of those, how many were successful? Failures?

- How do banks feel about lending money to finance the franchisees of the company?

- What are the average gross and net profits from the existing franchises?

- What kind of projects are there for additional outlets in the territory that you are considering?

- What kind of long-term prospects do they see for the company. Based upon what?

- Are the franchises subject to resale on the open market or must they be turned back to the company?

- What protection do you have against being "disenfranchised" if your efforts are very successful?

- What are the key competitive advantages that this franchise has over the competition?

Again, the idea is not to become a grand inquisitor and barrage the adversary with unsettling questions. What you are doing has two main goals:

1. You want to get some straight answers and clear information; 2. You want to put the franchisor on the defensive to increase your bargaining position. You do *not* want the negotiating session to be a confrontation. Therefore ask your questions courteously and, if you feel you are not getting a straight answer, leave the topic for now but don't forget about it. Return to it later.

This procedure has the additional benefit of qualifying the franchisor for you. If the franchisor grows impatient with your questions or tries to demean them as the utterances of a "greenhorn" you will be well advised to keep your checkbook in your pocket and look elsewhere for an opportunity. An ethical franchisor will offer you all the information you want to know. There is no real opportunity that won't hold up under examination.

Don't allow yourself to be misled. You are about to make a sizable investment that will affect your life and the life of your family. Therefore you are perfectly within your rights to ask all the questions that you feel need answering. And don't lie to yourself. If there is something that you don't understand don't pretend that you do. Just smile, excuse yourself and ask for clarification.

USING THE QUID PRO QUO OF NEGOTIATIONS

Once you have established the right climate for the negotiations by taking the initiative at the beginning of your talks, you are now ready to increase your leverage by means of an old tried-and-true method for getting negotiating results—the *quid pro quo*—in other words, "you scratch my back and I'll scratch yours." Obviously this method will work only if you have convinced yourself and your adversary that you are indeed an important part of the negotiations and that you could be very valuable to the franchisor. Look at it from the franchisor's point of view. If you were in his shoes, what would interest you about a prospective franchise buyer? Reliability for sure, financial solidity, the ability to learn quickly and responsiveness to company policies. Of course there are other more obvious attributes such as management ability, sales ability and the like, but all of the qualities we spoke of are important and if you have them they are negotiating points.

Use the *quid pro quo* to let your adversary know from the start that he cannot expect to get anything from you without giving something in return. Make it equally clear that you do not expect to be treated any differently. Don't forget that the franchisor will be making promises to you and sometimes he will not be able to do what he promised. This is to be expected. But your reaction can be either understanding or very demanding. Let him know by your attitude that you will not be pushed around but that neither will you be unreasonable in your demands on him.

SELL YOURSELF

Seasoned salesmen will tell you that one of the quickest ways to get close to a potential customer is to listen to him talk and then tell him back what he just told you. People tend to like people who agree with them and you can use this same technique in your negotiations with a franchisor.

Learn about the person you are talking with. Find out what he likes and doesn't like. Find out about his strengths and weaknesses. You can do this easily by talking to other franchise holders and comparing notes. Then get in there and sell yourself. Make your man like and respect you and, if you do, he will have a harder time resisting your demands. Regardless of what kind of business you are entering, it will never hurt to project yourself as a bright, attractive and competent personality. Even if your resumé is not complete and you lack what the franchisor thinks you should have in the way of financial backup, contacts or the like, the simple fact of his liking you will override many small objections. Again, put yourself in his shoes. If you were confronted by an individual who was bright, attentive and helpful, what would your reaction be? Probably you would like such a person and try to do what you could to help him.

USING "LEVERAGE"

Sometimes there will be a way that you can get a tremendous amount of leverage on the franchisor. It isn't usual but it sometimes happens that the franchisor really wants something that the franchisee has. For example, if you are a famous athlete you could use your public image to promote the franchisor. It doesn't take much imagination to see how a person with a public image could make a very good deal for himself by leveraging his assets into an asset for the front office.

Most of you don't have such a dramatic advantage, but it is also possible to leverage on a more mundane level. Let's assume that you were in a failing business but have ten years left on a lease on a very favorable piece of real estate in a high traffic area. It is very conceivable that a franchisor would make a sweet deal with you to take advantage of your lease. By the simple linking of your asset and his goals you could create a situation that was good for both of you.

Occasionally, you can use experience in a specialized field as a linkage to a better deal. This method is becoming more frequent as more and more of the so-called high-technology industries get into the franchise field.

The key to getting the most out of your strengths is careful self-evaluation. Learn to recognize your strengths and try to anticipate how your assets can be of special value to a franchisor. If you can convince him that you are right, you will undoubtedly be able to make the best possible agreement for yourself.

Summary of Points for Negotiating to Buy a Franchise:

- Research the field in which you want to buy a franchised business.

- Select the possible businesses for you and gather as much information about them as you can.

- Discuss the details with your lawyer and accountant.

- Generally, cost of franchise is not negotiable.

- Specific points to be negotiated:

  - Acceptance of yourself as a franchisee.

  - Accelerating success—measures to get into business and become profitable as soon as possible.

- Training—who will do it? How much will you get? Is it enough?

- Franchise agreement: Specifics can often be negotiated on a *quid pro quo* basis.

- Grace period—very common concession; allows the franchisee to get on his feet before heavy demands are made.

- Key negotiating techniques:

  - Put the franchisor on defensive by asking for information.

  - Project a self-confident, positive attitude.

  - Be prepared to give up certain benefits to get what you really want.

- Leverage:

  - Parlay a decided advantage into a more decided advantage.

  - Use something that you have that is valuable to franchisor.

19.

Negotiating to Buy an Independent Non-Franchised Business

Objectives:

- Importance of prior fact-finding

- Knowing the pros and cons of the business—how used in negotiations

- How to evaluate the time "worth" of the business—factors to consider

Much of the ground work we talked about for selecting a franchised business applies as well if you are interested in purchasing an independent going business. The key difference is that with an independent business you will have to do much more independent research. Also, the stakes will probably be higher as you will be "on your own" much more quickly when you buy a business from an independent.

The assumption has to be made that if you are thinking about buying an independent business you know something about the field and have at least a general idea of what to expect.

As with any unique entity, an independent business has both advantages and disadvantages. Unlike a franchise you do not have to step to anyone's tune but your own. You can do things your way and, if you have strong feelings about the way your business could be run, you will have the chance to put these ideas into action. There is no franchise fee or royalty with an independent business, and all the money that you earn you can keep. On the other hand there are some rather serious shortcomings. The first is that you are completely and totally on your own. If something is going wrong there is no home office to offer you backup advice. You will have to find that advice on your own and at your own expense. Another serious problem is that many small business owners become a slave to their businesses, devoting more time to it than is justified by the amount of money that they are taking home. Many of these people love what they are doing and don't seem to mind. But will *you* mind?

The problem is that a small business is very flexible, allowing the proprietor to take on more than one job. This kind of versatility is not practical in larger organizations but seems to be fairly common in small independently owned businesses. While this diversification of effort is not necessarily bad, it is misleading. It is misleading because small business owners often don't count their own labor and efforts when the time comes to put together a profit and loss statement. They don't realize that if they actually hired a clerk, typist, computer operator, shipping clerk or whomever, they would, in effect, not be showing much of a profit at all.

THE YOU FACTOR

For this reason it is extremely important that you ascertain the truth about the owner's input from the person who is selling a business. You might find out that the friendly fellow who is selling a busy laundromat is not actually selling a "management-free" cash business as he advertised. Instead he is really running a sweat shop for owners who are tied down twelve hours a day listening to customer complaints and fixing leaky valves.

Going into a business of your own is a heady and wonderful experience. But you should exercise extreme caution before you throw yourself into something that may well be much more than you bargained for. Look at it this way: If you had $100,000 to invest in a business and the present owner proved to you that you could earn 20% a year on your money, you should ask for more information before you sign on the dotted line. Is that 20% after you take out your salary or before? There is quite a big difference and if the figure includes your salary, the 20% figure is not as good as it sounded. After all, with today's high interest rates you can earn 10% by putting your money in high-grade corporate bonds. And so the additional 10% is probably much less than you could earn at your present job. In this case it would not only be ill advised for you to go into such a business (depending upon the growth potential of course), it could be downright foolish. After all, corporate bonds or other fixed income investments are very liquid and can be sold off within one or two business days. This is not true with a going business where it often takes months, and even longer, to find the right buyer.

Because of these shortcomings, the well-informed buyer of a business can generally wield considerable leverage but this is not a reason to pursue this choice. Unless you are very well informed and have some experience in the field, you are probably better off getting some experience before you buy an independent business.

THE KEY TO NEGOTIATING THE INDEPENDENT BUSINESS PURCHASE: FACT FINDING

Probably the most important single factor in determining whether an existing business is worth buying is the financial information contained in the company's books and records. Unless you are an accountant or have a great deal of experience in the business that you are buying, you are advised to have your accountants go over the books and explain their findings to you. Only by understanding the financial foundations of the business you are interested in will you be able to determine if it is worth your while and if it is worth the price that the owner is asking for it.

Then, too, there is another kind of fact-finding that isn't written down in books and ledgers. A good part of what you buy when you purchase a going business is called "good will." This means that you are paying for a business that has been in a set location for a number of years and has a following of satisfied customers. Naturally, good will is a fleeting and fickle commodity. The former owner is not promising that the customers that he has will come to you, but they probably will do just that. Still, there is no contract and part of your detective work will be to determine the reputation of the business in the neighborhood. If the business is a store, check out the customers and strike up a conversation with them. Find out what they like about the business and what they don't like. Find out how long they have been patronizing the business and how service could be improved. If the business is involved in a service or is a contractor to other businesses, put out some feelers in the trade and find out as much as you can about the business and the former owner. Did he pay his bills on time? Was he a reliable supplier? Is he generally well liked or do people do business with him simply because he always has the lowest price?

Finally, are you ready to evaluate the worth of the business, including the money and effort that you will have to put into it? Sit down with your accountant to see what you feel the business is really worth. Once you do that, try to arrange (at least in your own mind) the total expenses necessary for you to buy in and get into business and balance that against the books that the owner has shown you. Work with your accountant to project your yearly earnings and try to estimate as far as possible how much personal effort will be necessary. (The preceding statement isn't meant to imply that an individual in business should be concerned about long hours—these are an inevitability for all entrepreneurs—it is meant to determine if a profit could be earned without unreasonable personal demands on the owner.)

Once you have determined what the business is worth to you, you have reached the first step of your negotiations. You are now ready to sit down with the seller of the business and negotiate the terms of the sale.

WHAT TO NEGOTIATE

Clearly the price set on a business by a corporate franchisor is no more sacred than that set by a private individual who wants to sell his business at the best possible price. There are differences, however, and these differences should be considered. In general the price set by the franchisor is arrived at by some kind of standard formula. If the franchisor is reputable and business-minded, the figures that are set as value are based upon the worth of the franchisee's earning power as measured by various reporting systems. You can argue about the methods used, but generally the price can be justified by some kind of logic. This is not always the case with a private individual whose perception of the value of his business is inevitably tinged with emotion. The small business person has labored long hours at the business; he may well have built it up from nothing and he undoubtedly has seen it through the tough times. Therefore, it is a rare proprietor who can sit back and place an objective value.

This doesn't mean that you have to agree to the price that is set. You should understand how the seller of a business feels, and you should make a concerted effort not to deflate his ego when you negotiate the price down. Your best bet is to counter an unreasonable demand with straight cold business logic. Thus: "Mr. Seller, I know how you must feel about a business that you built up from scratch. But look here at my point of view. At the present asking price I would have to leave my money in this business for the next twenty years to get the same return that I could get by buying government bonds in only twelve years. And in this case I have to work for it. I am willing to accept a certain amount of risk for the prospect of growing with this business, but there have to be limits. At the figure I had in mind I could recoup my investment in ten years, which seems more than fair to me. What do you think?"

This approach asks the seller to justify his price without rubbing his nose in the fact that he has assigned a value without justification. When put in this light the seller either has to stick to his guns, in which case he will lose you as a prospect, or he will have to be more objective about the worth of his business.

By the way, it is very important to stress that if you pay too much for a going business, your chance of making it successful is almost zero. Most businesses are bought with a sizable down payment and monthly notes. These notes will be a regular fixed expense, in addition to rent, payroll, taxes and materials or supplies. If the notes are too high the only way that you will be able to pay them is to borrow heavily or else to *not* pay your other obligations. Either way you will be the loser. Again, we know that the flush of being in business for yourself can make you a little light-headed, but a word to the wise is sufficient. In business the numbers never lie. Unless you can make money on paper you won't make money in fact. If the terms are too tight for you, back off and walk away. There are people who make a living by selling a business at exorbitant prices to inexperienced but enthusiastic entrepreneurs, only to take them back when they default on their notes. If you can't make money in your own business there is really no advantage in doing it. You are really better off working for someone.

NEGOTIATING TERMS

Just as important as the price of the business are the terms of the sale. As above, these terms must be ones that you can live with reasonably. Don't let yourself be talked into monthly notes that are too high to handle using the previous year's receipts as your guide. In other words, don't be too ambitious in your projections of new business. Use last year's figures, and if you can't make it with them, either walk away or negotiate smaller monthly payments, or payments over a longer period of time. Your approach to the seller should be this: "Mr. Seller, I want to be fair with you. If I can't operate this business without financial hardship, it really would not be fair to either of us. The monthly figures that you propose are just too high. If I had two bad months I would be in deep trouble and my reserve would be wiped out. I want to do what's fair but I will not get involved unless I have a little more breathing room than you propose."

By using facts and figures you have removed the head-to-head nature of the negotiations and have enlisted the seller as your colleague. Instead of you against him, it is now you and he against the income statement.

WHAT ELSE IS NEGOTIABLE?

There are many details about the selling of a business that pass beyond the scope of this treatment. The terms of the notes or other negotiable instruments and the safeguards that relate to the protection of buyer and seller are best left to an experienced business lawyer. However, there are other matters that are important when a business changes hands, that need to be discussed and decided in advance.

Training: Every business requires certain special skills. Small businesses perhaps more than large ones definitely require specialized skills and knowledge of their owners. Don't assume that you can move right in and keep things rolling. It's impossible. The best way is to negotiate a transition period during which the former owner will stay with you, introduce you to his suppliers and customers and walk you through an average week or two weeks on the job. This might seem unnecessary or "Mickey Mouse," but it is a *very* important step. There are certain skills that only specialized experience can teach, and you can save yourself months of effort reinventing the wheel by watching someone who really knows what he is doing.

Former Owner as Consultant: This is an item that you might not use but which might be helpful in the negotiations. You should come to a per diem figure to be paid to the former owner if you need him to help you out with a problem in the business. The per diem rate should be high because the idea here is to massage the former owner's ego. Assume that the rate you set is $250 a day. Chances are he has never earned that much in a day since being in business. The fact that *you* recognized his true worth will build you up in his eyes and make him much easier to deal with on other issues.

If you do run into a problem and have to employ

him, the rate will still be cheap because there is no way on earth that you could ever hire a person who knows more about your business than the man who spent years running it.

All in all this is a good tactic as it allows you to keep in close touch with a valuable man who will always be very glad to hear from you.

Receivables, Liabilities, et al: A business is a living thing. At any one time there is always money owed and money due. The way that this money should be handled in terms of the sale of the business is an important part of the selling price. Once again, this is an area when precedent and experience are very important so be advised to depend on your attorney.

Sell Yourself: As with any kind of business transition, it will be easier if the former owner likes you and wants to work with you. Even if you think that he is a real dummy and has been running his business with stone age practices, be very careful to defer to him and ask his advice.

There is nothing that rankles a person more than somebody who thinks he knows *his* business better. If you have wise-guy tendencies make sure that you stifle them. Project a positive image to the former owner because as long as he is still on the scene he can only help you. There will be plenty of time to assert your own personality after the business passes to you.

ON STARTING A BUSINESS

Of all the ways to get into business, starting one

from scratch is at once the most exciting and the most treacherous. The start-up business has the highest rate of failure of all new businesses and its not hard to figure out why.

When you start from scratch you are responsible for *everything* from securing a place of business to ordering equipment, to prospecting business, to hiring employees and the list goes on and on and on and on. You will be called upon to negotiate with landlords, and suppliers and bankers and even prospective clients or customers. Unless you start with enough money you will develop catastrophic cash-flow problems because you will have no way of knowing what your cash flow will be. In short you will be sailing on uncharted waters and, unless you really have some experience and a good idea of what you are doing, you are advised to sit this one out.

The best advice that we can offer to anyone who is seriously thinking of starting a new business is something that almost nobody ever does. That is to hire a business consultant. Find someone in the same business that interests you and pick his brains. Whatever he charges you will be cheap because there is no way that you can duplicate first-hand experience. Another word of advice: most new start-ups are doomed from the first day they open up by a fatal flaw of location, poor positioning or insufficient working capital. So don't be afraid to take all the time you need to get ready. Of all the things that you will do in business, planning is far and away the cheapest.

Summary:

BUSINESS OWNERSHIP NEGOTIATION TACTICS

1. Buying non-franchised business. Buy the expertise of someone owning an existing related business.

2. Starting your own business:
   Make a plan. Go over every step leading to effective business implementation.

20.
A Summary of Negotiating for Success

PRINCIPLES AND SKILLS

As with any communication art, successful negotiating requires, above all else, a knowledge and an empathy for your fellow human beings. This is where our summary must begin. Unless you take an interest in what makes your adversary tick, you will not be able to negotiate with him very successfully. Ideally, this knowledge of people will come from your own experience in your present field of endeavor or in researching the field you want to enter. It can come from reading, and it can come also from talking with people you know who have a good deal of negotiating experience. In attempting to master a skill like negotiation it will serve you in good stead to remember this: the situations in which negotiating skills can serve you or your career are limitless—but in each case you will be negotiating with another person whose human side must be carefully considered if you are to be successful.

While there is no "right" way to negotiate for any specific goal, there are, however, several broad principles which can serve as your touchstones. For the sake of organization we have presented these principles in two categories that are here presented for your review:

SUMMARY I

GENERAL PRINCIPLES FOR SUCCESSFUL NEGOTIATIONS

1. *Be yourself:* If ten individuals set out to make themselves more effective negotiators, they will be successful if—and this is a big "if"—each of them develops his or her own approach and technique—one best suited to his or her own personality and not that of others. This principle of negotiation is absolutely essential. If it were possible for you to study the techniques of the world's greatest negotiators and analyze and explain what they are doing right, *you* would still not be a successful negotiator if you did not more than attempt to copy their methods. You could conceivably come up with a few useful things, but you would then have to modify these techniques to fit your own personality and your own way of doing things.

If you want to be a good negotiator, the first thing you must do is to believe in yourself and be convinced that you have within you the ability to turn another person to your way of thinking. If you lack this self-confidence, you will be unable to negotiate well no matter how much you learn or know about the techniques of the masters.

A wise negotiator will know himself or herself and learn to sense the flow of the negotiations. Then it becomes a matter of utilizing personality strengths or weaknesses to get the most of the perceived situation. It is possible, and common, to transform a strength into a weakness and vice versa. The key factor, however, is to make sure that the *tools* of your negotiations are really yours. You *must* use your own personality.

There is an ancient Oriental proverb that states that every person on earth is the best in the world at doing something. It is the problem of life to determine what you are best at! The same principle applies to negotiations. Naturally, everybody can't be the best, but everyone can be effective in his own way. The first obstacle to overcome is to find in your own mind the negotiating position in which you feel most comfortable.

By the way: you won't be able to fake it. If you think that you can't be a successful negotiator because you are not aggressive by nature, don't let that stop you. You can learn to be effective without being aggressive, and if you are honest with yourself it will work. However, if you try to become aggressive because you hope that will make you a better negotiator, you will fail.

You are your own laboratory. Study yourself and be frank about what you find. Then sit down with yourself and think candidly and openly how you can use your own personality to get the best negotiating results. You will be surprised at the vastness of your own capabilities.

2. *Be ethical:* This is a book about negotiating successfully in your business or career. Always remember that you are in business or professional life for a long time. Promises always come easier

than results. In the long run, your career will not be able to withstand erosions of confidence or credibility brought about by being deceitful or unreliable.

Don't be in too much of a hurry to achieve what you want. If you enter a negotiating session and, at the start, win nothing but your adversary's respect, you have gained a great deal. True, this is not the kind of gain that you can take to the bank today, but you will eventually see the rewards.

It takes a long time to build a reputation for fairness, honesty and reliability. Once won, it will serve as your most valuable negotiating strength. Turn the situation inside out. Would you rather strike a deal with a person whose reputation is above reproach for "x" number of dollars, or would you take a chance on a person who is known to be deceitful and unreliable for slightly better terms? Part of your negotiating repertoire must include a reputation you build by the way you deal with people.

Perspective is very important in keeping yourself on the right path. If you just keep in mind that no single business transaction is worth your entire career, you will have the proper perspective. While it takes a long time to build a reputation for reliability and honesty, it doesn't take that long to lose it. One slip is all you need to lose years of credibility. And once you lose your credibility with an adversary, it will be very difficult to regain it.

This is why it is so difficult to find jobs for ex-convicts. Prospective employers are afraid that they will revert to their former ways. This may not be fair to those who have paid their debt to society, but it is a fact of life and applies equally to people with a reputation for deceit or trickery.

According to a friend of ours, if you walk away

from a negotiating session with your dignity and reputation intact, you can chalk up a victory. In the realm of personal negotiations we would surely agree with him.

3. *Accentuate the positive:* This is a very important general principle. Negativism is bad *per se*. Always negotiate *for* something positive, never against something negative.

Negative negotiating will put your adversary in a defensive posture and will not be conducive to good communications. This type of approach can be perceived as an attack on your adversary, and he will retaliate by hitting you with something negative. You will then respond negatively and eventually you will get nowhere.

It is much more productive to take an approach that stresses the joint benefits of a positive alliance of purpose. You and your adversary are working together, moving forward together, prospering together. Just as a negative response yields a negative reaction, so does a positive appeal elicit the same in the adversary. Positive moves and impulses tend to be more communicative and effective than negative, and hence will move negotiations more smoothly and quickly.

Finally, a positive approach is the approach of the future. The future, after all, is where the benefits of any negotiations ultimately lie. A negative approach sullies and demeans the future and places a pall on the whole negotiating process. If you know that you are going to do well, you will not mind sharing a little more of the pie. If you think that you are going to wind up in dire straits, you will tend to become very tight and inflexible. This is simple human nature. Why not use it to your best interests by taking a positive approach!

4. *Clearly define your goals:* Personal negotiations are naturally much simpler than the large-scale negotiations of labor and management that we read about in the newspapers. However, they are similar in that they both have ramifications that reach beyond the issues being discussed. For example, let's assume that a corporation's chief negotiator includes triple time for Sunday work as part of a package to the union. He includes it because he knows that the company's present plan is adequate for all production needs and that Sunday shifts have never before been necessary. If the status quo continues, the negotiator has done well. He has included a juicy plum for the union which doesn't really mean anything since it will never be implemented. However, what if, by bad planning the plant *did* have to put on Sunday workers to meet new production demands? And what happens if failure to meet these demands would mean losing key accounts to competitors? Then the triple time for Sunday work suddenly becomes a very serious concession—possibly one that could mean the difference between profit and loss for the corporation.

The way to avoid this kind of situation is to carefully think out the ramifications of all negotiated points. This applies to your personal negotiations as well as to the large-scale talks of a professional negotiator.

Clear thinking is highly important in first determining whether your negotiating goals are realistic. Before entering negotiations, be sure to get straight in your own mind *exactly* what you want to achieve, not *approximately*. Note that you will never get *exactly* what you want, but unless you know just what it is you want, you will not be able to approach your goals effectively. You don't have to determine the appropriateness or correctness of your goals in a vacuum. By all means consult with others in the same field and get all the opinions and facts that you can.

The next step is to evaluate your goals in terms of whether or not they are really beneficial to you in the long run. If you are negotiating for a change from sales to management, you might win job security and a lessening of work pressures for a short term. In the long run you might be much more successful in sales once the contacts you have cultivated mature to full potential. In business nothing happens in a vacuum. Changing one factor will change other factors, and it is part of the negotiator's job to anticipate, as far as possible, what these changes will mean in terms of long-range objectives.

The final and perhaps the most obvious reason for employing clear thinking to define your negotiating goal is that it allows you to communicate your goals more easily. While this, to repeat, seems obvious, the fact remains that unless *you know* what you want, you won't be able to *tell somebody else* about it. Don't ever depend upon your adversary to tell you what you want. This would be like going into a restaurant and telling the waiter to bring you something "good to eat." By clarifying your goals for yourself, you also will clarify them for your adversary, and in this way you will achieve faster and more productive communication.

Unclear or undefined expectations are the deadly enemy of any kind of negotiations. Sessions fueled by such hazy objectives are inevitably doomed to become highly emotional personality clashes that, in the end, benefit nobody.

SUMMARY II

ON BECOMING A BETTER NEGOTIATOR

Key Points to Remember:

1. *Don't hurry.* Find your own tempo, set your own pace, and don't be pushed from it. Negotiating is an important activity and therefore all the details that make up a negotiating session are also important. Different individuals feel more comfortable working at different rates of speed. Some are slow, courteous and thorough. Some feel more comfortable getting down to business and discussing each point until resolution. These differences in pace are inevitable and there is absolutely nothing that you can do about it. Therefore, if you find yourself negotiating with an adversary who is pushing you too hard for a quick agreement, you have to learn to stand your ground and let him respect *your* internal clock. Very few issues *must* be settled right now! Most can wait and therefore you don't have to feel guilty or ashamed of advancing at your own pace.

By the same token, don't allow yourself to be railroaded into accepting a point you don't understand. If something is difficult for you to grasp, apologize for your "slowness" and ask for clarification. After a while you may find that many of these "quick points" really aren't points at all and will not stand the test of being explained. Even if they do, you still have every right to understand each issue at your own pace and in your own words.

2. *Make sure you have the facts to back up each of your objectives.* "Don't go off half-cocked" is the old saw used to describe this sound bit of negotiating advice. Your adversary always has the right to ask "Why?" And you have the obligation to tell him. "Because that's what I want" or "That's the way it is" is not an acceptable rationale for the negotiator.

It is said that "there is nothing more stubborn than facts." Similarly, and in logical sequence, there is nothing more convincing than facts. There is no better argument than a skillfully constructed argument documented with facts.

This means that you will have to do some preparation for your negotiations, and you should use your preparations as a way of building as strong a case for yourself as you can. The more information you present, the stronger the case you will make. If your adversary is already cognizant of the information you are presenting, he will respect you as a colleague who knows as much as he knows. If he isn't familiar with the facts you are presenting, he will be less likely to challenge and oppose you, because now *he*—not you—is treading on unfamiliar territory.

Often there are no facts. Even in these cases you can prepare strong positions for yourself by documentation with *opinions* based on similar situations, or with opinions from experts or others whose reputations are known and respected.

It is very important to show your adversary that you are a person who "knows what he is talking about."

There is also a sobering and rationalizing effect in keeping your sessions in the arena of facts rather than expressing irrational cravings and desires.

191

3. *Try to keep some flexibility in each position you take.* Do not negotiate yourself out on a limb. Inflexibility is not a good trait because it cuts off a certain amount of creative thought. This can have a disastrous effect on negotiations because what you're doing is telling your adversary, "It's my way or no way at all!" And that will certainly incense your opponent.

Being flexible doesn't mean that you've got to give up your principles or put your goals aside. It only means that you are not locking yourself into a single way of approaching a problem. A flexible person will be able to see a problem from a number of different angles and possibly come out with a solution which is actually better than the approach selected initially.

Being inflexible is dangerous. It can make your adversary aggressively defensive and can also cause you to maneuver yourself into a position from which there is absolutely no turning back. Never allow yourself to assume that some demands are "non-negotiable." Everything is negotiable under certain circumstances. Being inflexible will only stop you from ever reaching this new ground.

4. *Always look for the real motive behind your adversary's words.* Continually ask yourself: What did he mean by that?

There is an old joke about two psychiatrists who meet casually one morning in the halls of the hospital where they work. One psychiatrist greets the other by saying, "Good morning, Herb." The other psychiatrist scratches his head and asks himself: "Humm, I wonder what he meant by that?"

While this slightly overstates the case, it is nevertheless important to consider each and every thing an adversary says to you, complete with pauses, facial expressions, tone of voice and body language (see Chapter 15) and then to evaluate what he is getting at. As you gain more and more experience as a negotiator you will begin to perceive the meaning that actually lies behind the words. What does it mean if your adversary suddenly looks away from you when you are discussing a key point? Is he ashamed of his attitude on this point? And if so, is this the time to stiffen your approach and take advantage of his equivocation? If your adversary says something outlandish, is he looking for an argument or is he trying to make a joke and loosen up the talks?

The point here is that communication takes place both within the words used, and "between" the words. It is up to you to understand this and to become as skilled as possible in both kinds of communication.

5. *Remember that money is not everything.* There are two ways in which blind faith in the "Almighty Dollar" can result in unsatisfactory negotiations.

The first way is to concentrate too much effort on the purely monetary or financial side of the issue. This is particularly important to readers of this book who are executives or who want to operate their own business. Each year surveys reveal that more and more Americans are under-employed—that is, working at jobs that are not challenging or satisfying enough. Yet *many* of these same individuals are adequately paid for their work.

Money is important. It is very important. But it is not *the* most important issue and never will be. Money exists as a tool and as a measure of success. If you gear up to address only the issue of "how much," you may find that you are either taking for granted or neglecting issues that could have a greater effect on your life and welfare. Recently a friend of ours in the advertising business got a job offer. He negotiated a salary twice the amount he was making as an art director of a large, prominent agency. He was ecstatic. He crowed that people who were at his old agency twice as long as he, didn't make the kind of money he was now making. But there was a very important fly in the ointment. His new employer, a small agency with a reputation for creative genius, demanded that he put in long hours, weekends and many road trips. Within a few weeks our friend was re-evaluating his decision, and within two months he was back at his old job and glad to be there.

So while money is always one of the issues, don't be blinded to other issues that are at least as important.

Another way in which money can lead you astray is by assuming that it is the main focus of your adversary's attention. Believe it or not, people are sometimes motivated by some things other than money. Chief among them: loyalty, ego, pride, and the need to be independent. While these instances are not quite so common, they are not altogether uncommon, and you should allow for their possibility. Nothing will pull an adversary's nose out of joint more quickly than to have a deeply embedded pet motivation demeaned by you as being insignificant or unimportant.

6. *Be alert to your adversary's priorities.* Don't assume that they are the same as yours.

Just as you should not assume that money is the one and only motivating factor, you should also guard against making other assumptions. Ideally, you should start each negotiating session with only one assumption: namely that common ground can be reached by you and your adversary. However, that is as far as it should go. Unless they are based on good solid research, assumptions will not do much to advance your purposes. Quite the contrary can be true. If you are really interested in a single area of the negotiation, you might assume quite naturally that your adversary will also be interested in this same area. Therefore you will tend to bear down on this point, and your adversary in his turn might turn defensive and lock horns with you. The point is that by your assumption you have actually "picked the fight." Had you proceeded in a less determined manner, you might have detected a certain lack of concentration on your adversary's part. This would have told you that what was very important to you was just a formality to him. By skillfully feigning the same disinterest, you can get what you most want. But you can't do it by making assumptions. You have to prepare and keep aware and have your goals clearly in mind.

7. *Learn to listen.* Don't just wait for your turn to speak. Remember that there are two reasons why it is important to be a good listener. First, of course, it is to gain information and insights into your adversary. However, there is another reason just as important: listening well tells the other person that you are interested in him and that you think what he is saying is important and worthwhile.

Listening is an important aid to communication

for both of these reasons. An adversary who is convinced that you are listening to him will make special efforts to be clear and straightforward. A good way to convince your adversary that you are listening is to ask intelligent questions. Keep the questions on the topic he is discussing rather than changing the subject. Even if you are bursting to tell your side, remain calm and collected and wait for your adversary to make his point.

In effect you are doing two things. You are learning to listen to your adversary. But you are also proving to your adversary that you are listening, and that you are not summarily discounting his viewpoints. This saves his ego, and it also smooths the way for negotiating.

8. *Learn to control your emotions.* Don't panic or lose your cool.

Venting of the emotions is a necessary part of life; but not of business. Every business or professional person who takes himself seriously is happy about what he is doing and is proud of his professionalism. Emotional outbursts simply are not professional. In fact, they fly in the face of the self-image that most professional and business people have. Remember that you are a professional, and you will tend to act like a professional. Remember also that it is not the end of the world if your negotiations are not successful this time. Nobody likes to negotiate with a desperate person. If you are desperate you must exert extra effort not to appear that way. Sometimes your negotiations will not work out, and you will have to summon up all your self-respect and dignity and walk away.

On the more positive side, you can often salvage a

situation by remaining calm in the face of adversity. There are times when you will have to settle for less than you would like because of pressures beyond your control. Such situations are always worse if you panic and lose the ability to think clearly in the midst of your negotiations.

The self-image of the good negotiator should be very similar to that of an emergency room doctor. Many of the situations that come up will be potentially emotional and unsettling. The doctor remains professional and unemotional because this is the state of mind that allows him to do his best work. It is the same with a good negotiator. He has to work to develop the toughness of mind to persevere even when the events are personally very upsetting.

9. *Don't be greedy.* There is an old saying among the investment community on Wall Street that bulls can make money and bears can make money, but pigs never do. There is a lot of good advice in this statement.

By their very nature, negotiations are compromises. Even a young child learns that choices must always be made. A viable choice is either/or—but rarely both. Greed is a terrible quality for a negotiator, because it is an emotion that overrides reason. And whenever that happens, the negotiations seldom end well.

The fact that you are greedy will most likely not go unnoticed by your adversary, and you can hardly hope to be respected for it. By definition, a greedy person wants more than he deserves, and this is patently unfair. A greedy person therefore carries the wrong attitude into negotiations, and is more apt to incite bad feelings and distrust in his adversary.

There is also another more practical and self-serving reason for not being greedy: in the long run it will end up meaning much *more* for you. For example, it might happen that because of an unusual amount of leverage, you can tilt a certain transaction to your benefit. You indeed have the opportunity to be greedy and to realize your gains immediately. If you do this, one of two things will probably come to pass. Either you will gain yourself the permanent mistrust of your adversary who will be wary of ever doing business with you in the future; or possibly the deal will be weighted so far in your favor that the adversary might not be able to honor his obligations. This latter case is very familiar when relatively inexperienced people purchase businesses at prices that are so inflated that their efforts to run these businesses are doomed from the start. In either case there is no long-term advantage as you have lost an associate and business contact, and your short-term windfall loses significance when viewed from the perspective of the passing years.

10. *Learn to study and understand personalities.* This is perhaps the most enjoyable and edifying of all the summarizing points. Don't accept people at face value. Study them and try to understand what motivates them. If a person comes on rough-and-tough, what does this mean? If a person is continuously late for appointments or frequently mispronounces your name, are you sure that these actions aren't being done purposely to throw you off balance? This is a fairly open-ended endeavor. You can study people (yourself included) with your eyes, ears and brain, or you can read social psychology and other authors for possible insights into the human

animal. The point here is not to take people at face value. Play psychological detective and you will be amazed at the advantages that can accrue.

11. *Be a gracious winner.* Being a good winner is every bit as important as being a good loser. If you are boorish or insensitive and humiliate an adversary, you will be assured of having an enemy for life. If you keep it up, it is only a matter of time before you will have to pay for your insensitivity. A good negotiator will treat a victory not as the vanquishing of his adversary, but as a joint victory. He will celebrate the success that the two of them have together and will toast the resolution of their differences. He will make his adversary feel that any extra compromises will be made up by their future mutual prosperity.

Being a good winner costs you nothing but pays big dividends. It assures that you will maintain a harmonious working relationship with your adversary, and this increases the possibility of future business transactions and referrals.

12. *Get it in writing.* There is a magical transformation that occurs when something is "signed on the dotted line." Even if it is only an informal agreement, it is a useful and effective tool as it shows intent at the same time as it cements the negotiated agreement.

You needn't feel that an adversary will be insulted by asking for your agreement reduced to writing. If the intention is there, there will be no resistance to seeing your agreement in written, binding form.

Also, the preliminary agreement is a quick and easy path to the more formal agreement that will come later. Indeed, in the very act of reducing an agreement to writing, issues are often clarified and better understood by both parties.

In the event that you are negotiating with a larger organization that already has legal forms prepared, you can agree to sign a letter of intention and ask for time to go over formal terms with your attorney. Such a letter will clarify your intent without obligating you to clauses and other boilerplate conditions that you do not yet understand or agree to.

13. *Prepare, prepare, prepare* . . . This final summarizing step should perhaps have been the first. It cannot be stressed enough that you will never be a good negotiator unless you prepare diligently for each negotiation. This means that you must be able to research your area of expertise, give some attention to the physical details of the time and place of the negotiating session, try to analyze the personality of yourself vis-à-vis your adversary and take the time to think out your goals and the means to achieving them. You must then be able to prepare documented material, bring in additional people to help your case. And finally, you must actually practice your tactics before the main event. Does this sound like a tremendous amount of work? Well, it is!

Remember that negotiating will be used at very important times of your life. The results of these negotiations can have a vast influence on the kind of life you have, the satisfaction you get from your work, and the financial rewards you receive. In short, these negotiating sessions can actually affect your happiness and self-fulfillment. If that isn't worth preparing for, what is?

Index

AMF, 35

Recommended MENTOR and SIGNET Books

Buy them at your local

bookstore or use coupon

on next page for ordering.

Recommended Reading from SIGNET and MENTOR